Sermons
for
Church
Year
Festivals

Donald L. Deffner

CPH.
SAINT LOUIS

Copyright © 1997 Concordia Publishing House
3558 S. Jefferson Avenue, St. Louis, MO 63118-3968
Manufactured in the United States of America

Library of Congress Cataloging-in-Publication Data

Deffner, Donald L.
    Sermons for church year festivals / Donald L. Deffner.
        p.   cm.
    Includes bibliographical references and index.
    ISBN 0-570-04975-X
    1. Festival-day sermons. 2. Church year sermons. I. Title.
BV4254.3.D44   1997
252′.6–dc21   97-2350

1   2   3   4   5   6   7   8   9   10   06   05   04   03   02   01   00   99   98   97

To my friend
Dr. Reuben W. Hahn
pioneer
in the church's campus ministry

Acknowledgments

I hope you will find some adaptable stuff in these pages. Make it your own. Add to it from your personal pastoral experience. And then pass it on.

I applaud Jessica Wilmarth (†) for her usual outstanding work at the computer; Wayne Morton for many helpful suggestions; and Mervin A. Marquardt, David Koch, and Wilbert Rosin for their editorial expertise.

In what follows I credit P.H.D. Lang, Edward W. Wessling, and Richard Lischer for helpful source material. As noted, some of the material reprinted from *Lent: A Time for Renewal* is based on sermon studies by Gerhard Aho and Richard Kapfer.

Some sermons are adapted from material by the author in *The Concordia Pulpit* (St. Louis: Concordia Publishing House): "How Do You Start Your Day?" adapted from *Concordia Pulpit, 1989,* 1-4. "Are You Ready?" adapted from *Concordia Pulpit, 1978,* 3-8. "Are You Standing in the Doorway?" adapted from *Concordia Pulpit, 1978,* 8-14. "The Wounded Healer Returns to Restore Us," adapted from *Concordia Pulpit, 1990,* 76-80. "Tomorrow We'll Be There," adapted from *Concordia Pulpit, 1977,* 19-22. "Christmas—As a Little Child," adapted from *Concordia Pulpit, 1977,* 22-27. "Is Yours a Life of 'Practical Atheism'?" adapted from *Concordia Pulpit, 1980,* 91-94. "The Greatest News You Ever Heard," adapted from *Concordia Pulpit, 1980,* 94-100. "Are You Living the 'Ascended' Life?" adapted from *Concordia Pulpit, 1976,* 108-13. "Wake Up, Dry Bones!" adapted from *Concordia Pulpit, 1990,* 81-84.

Some sermons are adapted from material by the author in *Lent: A Time for Renewal* (St. Louis: Concordia Publishing House, 1989): "Are You on a Power Trip? 85-87; "Are You Standing in the Semicircle?" 109-12; "Are You a Spectator Christian?" 113-16; "Here We Stand—or Here We Go?" 93-96.

Some illustrations are from Richard Andersen and Donald L. Deffner, *For Example: Illustrations for Contemporary Preaching* (St. Louis: Concordia Publishing House, 1977).

Some illustrations are from Donald L. Deffner, *Seasonal Illustrations for Preaching and Teaching* (San Jose: Resource Publications, Inc. 160 E. Virginia Street #290, San Jose, California 95112–5876). Special thanks go to Resource Publications, Inc., for permission to quote.

Some illustrations are from Donald L. Deffner, *At Life's End,* (St. Louis: Concordia, 1995); *At the Death of a Child: Words of Comfort and Hope* (St. Louis: Concordia, 1993); *The Best of Your Life Is the Rest of Your Life* (Nashville: Abingdon, 1977); *Bold Ones on Campus: A Call for Christian Commitment* (St. Louis: Concordia, 1973); *The Bright Red Sports Car and Other Stories* (St. Louis: Concordia, 1993); *The Possible Years: Thoughts After Thirty on Christian Adulthood* (St. Louis: Concordia, 1973); *Prayers for People Under Pressure* (Milwaukee: Northwestern Publishing House, 1992); *The Unlocked Door and Other Stories* (St. Louis: Concordia, 1994; see also *The Secret Admirer and Other Stories* [St. Louis: Concordia, 1994]); *Windows into the Lectionary: Seasonal Illustrations for Preaching and Teaching* (San Jose, California: Resource Publications, Inc., 1996); *You Say You're Depressed? How God Helps You Overcome Anxieties* (Nashville: Abingdon, 1976).

Some illustrations are from Walter B. Knight, *Three Thousand Illustrations for Christian Service* (Grand Rapids: Wm. B. Eerdmans Publishing Company, 1947).

Contents

Scriptural Index

Isaiah 9:6
    The Nativity of Our Lord (Christmas Eve)

Ezekiel 37:1–3, 11–14
    Pentecost/Whitsunday

Hosea 5:15–6:2
    Fourth Sunday in Advent

Matthew 3:1–12
    Third Sunday in Advent

Matthew 20:26
    Ash Wednesday

Matthew 24:37–44
    Second Sunday in Advent

Luke 2:1–20
    The Nativity of Our Lord (Christmas Day)

Acts 1:8
    Reformation Day

Romans 3:24–25
    Good Friday

Romans 13:11–14
    First Sunday in Advent

1 Corinthians 9:22
    The Epiphany of Our Lord—January 6

1 Corinthians 10:16–17
    Maundy Thursday

1 Corinthians 15:1–11
    The Resurrection of Our Lord

Philippians 1:23–26
    All Saints' Day—November 1
        or
    Commemoration of the Faithful Departed—November 2

Hebrews 4:14–5:10
    Good Friday or Easter Eve

Hebrews 5:7–9
    The Ascension of Our Lord

Preface

"Topical" Sermons

Some preachers may designate the messages which follow as "topical" sermons. I affirm that fact and in the same breath challenge the pejorative note often implied in the term "topical." Indeed, I would like to redeem "topical" preaching, if by that we mean "sermons with a single, clear idea."

The great preacher John Henry Jowett once stated:

> No sermon is ready for preaching, nor ready for writing out, until we can express its theme in a short, pregnant sentence as clear as crystal. I find the getting of that sentence the hardest, the most exacting, and the most fruitful labor in my study. To compel oneself to fashion that sentence, to dismiss every word that is vague, ragged, ambiguous, to think oneself through to a form of words that defines the theme with scrupulous exactness—this is surely one of the most vital and essential factors in the making of a sermon; and I do not think any sermon ought to be preached or even written, until that sentence has emerged, clear and lucid as a cloudless moon. (*The Preacher, His Life and Work*. New York: Doran, 1912, 133.)

The error in not developing that "one clear idea" is that the preacher may try to "cover" (rather than uncover!) every verse in the text, assuming that such an approach is "expositional preaching." Or, the sermonizer may wander over all three lessons for the day, trying to do "liturgical justice" to them, rather than correlating the propers, but sticking to one central homiletical concept.

Henry Mitchell also affirms the "main idea" principle in sermon organization. "If real communication rather than a show of erudition is the goal, one good idea will be a quite satisfying achievement." (*The Recovery of Preaching* [New York: Harper and Row, 1977], 43.)

And Fred Craddock notes that the ability to capture the meaning of the text in one sentence "marks a genuine achievement, rewarded not only by a sense of satisfaction but by a new appetite for the next task: the sermon itself." (*Preaching* [Nashville: Abingdon Press, 1985], 122.)

To those who disdain topical preaching, I contended in *Compassionate Preaching: A Primer/Primer in Homiletics* (Fort Wayne: Concordia Seminary Press, 1991, 78) that there is such a thing as bad exegetical/expositional preaching. Some of the marks of that are

- Too much exegesis dragged into the pulpit
- Dull verse-by-verse commentary on text
- Presumption that the sheer statement of Bible truth equals communication
- People often are left to make their own application
- A rambling over several textual ideas, failing to focus on one central theme.

I pointed out that there also is such a thing as bad topical preaching. Its marks include

- Alluding to the text without developing it
- Weak on biblical content
- Long on "religious"/moral talk.

In between these two extremes I put *good* exegetical/expositional preaching and *good* topical preaching—which are one and the same! This type of sermon is biblical and fully textual, yet it addresses one clear theme instead of wandering around. The exegesis is implicit, and the interpretation of the text is thorough. Plus, both are applied to life in the light of that "one, clear idea."

Richard R. Caemmerer said that the preacher can get 19 different sermons on one text. "But you will be preaching on this text again. Today focus on one aspect of the text."

That is what I have sought to do. And I have attempted to provide a fresh tack or different direction in preaching at specific occasions, also using free texts. But though sometimes "topical," my first and foremost objective still has been biblical/textual preaching. And it has focused on the "one, clear idea" succinctly stated in a Law/Gospel, problem/resolution theme.

How Do You Start Your Day?

Romans 13:11-14

A realtor in California spoke of his anxiety at an impending open heart surgery—until he saw 27 other people in line at the hospital waiting for the same operation. The surgery was successful, and now a number of the heart patients even have their own softball team in Walnut Creek, California. The realtor says he has learned to live life differently now. He has learned to "put on Christ anew" each day, with heartfelt thanks to God. His first words every morning are, "Thank you, Lord, for another day."

Have you learned how to live that way—to "put on Christ" with thankfulness and expectation each day of your life? Today is the first day of a new church year, the beginning of the Advent season. We look forward to the coming of the Christ Child at Christmas time in just a few short weeks. Are you ready to prepare a manger in your heart to receive the Christ Child—and then to live with thankfulness and expectation each day of your life?

My theme: <u>Although we often permit ourselves to be squeezed into the world's mold, God calls us to "put on Christ" (v. 14) every day.</u>

Squeezed into the World's Mold

The trouble is, you and I often get sidetracked. We fail to heed Paul's words in Romans, "Don't let the world around you squeeze you into its own mould, but let God re-mould your minds from within, so that you may prove in practice that the Plan of God for you is good, meets all His demands and moves toward the goal of true maturity" (Rom. 12:2, *Letters*).

What are the ways the world tries to squeeze us into its own mold? Paul calls these temptations "the deeds of darkness." He says we should not live in "sexual immorality and debauchery." Though we may not engage in overt acts of evil, are our minds always pure? A psychiatric nurse in San Diego tells of a woman in a mental hospital, roped to her bed all day long, screaming out obscenities from morning till night. The patient had been a pastor's wife for 30 years, devoted to the Lord, but the environment around her—including the mass media of our day—evidently had made its impact on her subconscious mind.

Though you may not say vile words or act out unseemly behavior, do you think those things?

Paul also warns us about "dissension and jealousy." When was the last time you quarreled with someone? Can you honestly say you have never been jealous when another person got a higher score or more money than you did? Although you didn't actually say anything, what were you thinking?

Will the real "you" please stand up?

Yale psychiatrist Robert Jay Lifton tells of a teacher friend who envisages himself wearing a number of masks that he can put on or take off. As he recalls the books he has read with accounts of every kind of crime and sin, he adds, "For me, there's not a single act I cannot imagine myself committing." (*Boundaries* [New York: Random House, Inc., 1969], 44-46, 96-101)

Could you say that? Will the real you please stand up?

Perhaps you say to yourself, "I'm not really given to any of those things that the text is talking about." But when the Holy Spirit searches your heart, you can see the ways in your life that the world squeezes you into its own mold. What are the ways you fail to "put on Christ," the ways you fall short of living a daily life of thankfulness to God and expectation of his imminent coming?

When we are utterly honest with ourselves, we sigh like the penitent, "Lord, be merciful to me, a sinner." And we confess with Paul, "I know that nothing good lives in me, that is, in my sinful nature. For I have the desire to do what is good, but I cannot carry it out" (Rom. 7:18).

Putting on Christ

But there's also Good News for you from God's Word today. Listen: "Our salvation is nearer now than when we first believed ... the day is almost here" (Rom. 13:11-12). So "if we claim to be without sin, we deceive ourselves and the truth is not in us. If we confess our sins, he is faithful and just and will forgive us our sins and purify us from all unrighteousness" (1 John 1:8-9).

When you and I truly repent by the power of the Holy Spirit, God forgives our sins because of the death and resurrection of Jesus Christ. That's what we prayed for in the collect for today: "Stir up, we implore you, your power, O Lord, and come that by your protection we may be rescued from the threatening perils of our sins and be saved by your mighty deliverance." And then we exulted in the Gradual, "Rejoice greatly, O daughter of Zion! Shout, daughter of Jerusalem! See, your King comes to you, righteous and having salvation."

To us—forgiven and cleansed by Christ's death—God says, "Put on the armor of light ... Clothe yourselves with the Lord Jesus Christ." Ah—but how do we do that?

A Christian couple planning to sell their home to a black physician and his wife received threatening phone calls from their neighbors. One wailed, "How could you do this to us?"

The woman selling the home said, "We're simply doing what Christ would do."

Her irritated caller responded, "But he isn't here today!"

Christ isn't here today?

Christ *is* here today—in you and in me as baptized and redeemed children of God. When we catch the mind of Christ and by the power of the Spirit put on his character and traits and likeness, we *do* learn to live daily with thankfulness and expectation. We make his very presence known by the way in which we live among other people.

A missionary in the interior of China was just beginning to tell the story of Jesus to a group of people. A few minutes had passed when one of the natives said, "Oh, yes, we knew him; he used to live here."

Somewhat surprised, the missionary said, "No, he lived centuries ago in another land."

The man still insisted that he had seen Jesus, saying, "Not so! He lived in this village, and we knew him." Then they showed him the grave of a medical missionary who had lived, served, healed, and died in that community. (*Seasonal Illustrations,* 87)

Would people say that of you after you are gone? Would they say, "We remember her Christ-like character, for when she entered a room the fragrance of Christ came in with her"? Or "When he came into the office, somehow the whole place just seemed different"? When people look at you, do they see Christ shining right through you, like a beautiful stained-glass window?

The Gospel is communicated by a person who not only speaks it but also lives it. Scripture says, "What kind of people ought you to be? You ought to live holy and godly lives as you look forward to the day of God and speed its coming" (2 Peter 3:11–12).

Dr. Robert Oppenheimer once said, "The best way to send an idea is to wrap it up in a person." (Halford E. Luccock, *Communicating the Gospel* [New York: Harper and Brothers, 1954], 100) And that's what God did in the Incarnation. The Word became flesh and dwelt among us. And that's what you do when you "put on Christ" each day where you live and work and play, when his Word feeds your mind and his sacraments give life to your soul.

If I asked you suddenly to remember five good sermons you have heard in your life, you might have a hard time remembering them. But if I asked you to name five persons who had really "put on Christ" and through whom God had really touched you, I'm sure you could point right away to a parent, an aunt, a grandfather, a teacher. In the same way, as you share the love of God in Jesus Christ by your words and your actions, God can shine through you to bring others to "put on Christ."

That is my question to you. Are you, as Luther said, a "little Christ" wherever you go? Do people see in you more of the world or of God's Word? Do your non-Christian friends say, "Oh, Bill/Mary isn't all that different from us after all, even though he/she is a Christian. He gets loaded just like we do at a party. She enjoys a dirty joke as much as we do. They quarrel and cut each other down just like anyone else." Or do they say, "There's something different about those Christians. Look how they love one another! They really have a faith to live by. I want that faith, too."

Then we can direct them to the Author and Finisher of our faith, our Lord Jesus Christ. We can encourage them to "put him on" through Baptism and to receive the Eucharist joyfully every time it's offered. We can encourage them to search the Scriptures daily to know his will and plan for their lives. We can help them develop a much richer prayer life and seek out the fellowship of other Christians a good deal more.

The Advent season has begun once again. It's a time for living in the forgiveness of sins that God offers you daily through the death of his beloved Son. It's a time to get ready for Christ's return. It's a time to be thankful and expectant as we look forward to the celebration of his coming in the flesh for our salvation.

May the joy of that expectation be yours as you get up each morning! For that's the way to start your day.

Are You Ready?

Matthew 24:37-44

What were you doing Friday afternoon at 2:00 P.M.? Imagine someone had come to you exactly at that time and had said, "Stop what you are doing now."

And you had said, "But I'm not done with this yet."

And the person said again, "Stop now."

And you protested, "But it's only 2:00 o'clock! I have several hours to go yet this afternoon."

"Stop now," said the figure.

And you put down what you were doing and walked with the person and asked, "Will I be able to finish this later?"

"No."

"You mean I won't be able to pick up where I left off?"

"No."

"But where are you taking me?" you asked in anxiety.

"It's a long way off," said the figure. "Come on. This is the way."

"But I had such great plans for the weekend!"

"Come along," was the reply.

"Can't I go back for a moment?"

"No."

"But just for a minute, just one little minute, only to …"

"No! Come on!"

I think you know who the figure was—or could have been: Death.

Our text for today recounts some of our Lord's words towards the end of his ministry. He speaks of the end of the world and the need to be ready for it. Even as in the days of Noah, when the normal course of life was going on and the flood suddenly came, so it will be business as usual in people's lives when the trumpet sounds and all earthly life as we know it suddenly ceases to exist.

If we had known the hour, Christ says, we, like a house-owner expecting a burglar, would have been ready for it with a burglar alarm system and police waiting inside with guns drawn. But "you do not know on what day your Lord will come" (v. 42) he affirms. And so we are to watch (v. 42) and "be ready, because the Son of

Man will come at an hour when you do not expect him" (v. 44).

We consider this sobering theme this morning: <u>Because of our sinful nature, we are often inclined to be unprepared for Christ's return. The watchful Christian, however, waits for Christ's coming in joyful hope, not fear.</u> We will consider the following points:

    I. The need for preparation and

   II. Our spirit of preparation:

        A. Living in the present tense, and

        B. Living in hope, not fear.

The Need for Preparation

Christ will come when life is "business as usual."

A man walked into a restaurant for a cup of coffee. The room was moderately filled; an air of listlessness prevailed. People chatted; cups were filled; some loners gazed at their cups or out the window in silence. The man said the scene struck him like a "lot of people just sitting around waiting for Judgment Day." The ennui, the boredom, the same-old-routine aspect may give that impression, but I'm sure many of those people weren't thinking of Judgment Day at all—much less were they ready for it.

If there were a devils' council in hell at which the demons were conferring on how to best fulfill their evil task, I can hear one saying, "I will go to the earth and tell everyone that the Bible is a myth." Another says, "I will tell people there is no God, no Savior, no hell, no heaven." Another, "No, we must be more clever than that. People won't quite believe those lines. Why not tell people instead that these things are all true, but there really is no hurry. Judgment Day hasn't come for thousands of years and is not about to come in the next five minutes. So take your time!" I think I know whose plan was decided upon, for it has been working until this very day! That advice, however, is the opposite of our Lord's words here to us today: "Keep watch ... Understand this ... Be ready."

The grandmother on Christmas Day who frets while waiting for the family to arrive for dinner is not going to be nearly as ready as the grandmother who bastes the turkey in the kitchen and only now and then listens for the car coming into the driveway. All of the virgins in the next chapter of Matthew were sleeping while they waited for the bridegroom, but only some of them were prepared. You cannot always be looking heavenward for the personal appearance of our Lord, but it is possible for you to be prepared and ready for his coming.

People outside this church building are watching, ready for things that are about to happen. The highway patrol is watching the traffic. Nurses are watching patients in intensive care units in the hospital. Firefighters are listening for a bell. Ambulance attendants are sitting, ready for the phone to ring. On the other hand, a sleepy air-control tower operator has been responsible for two planes crashing in midair. A negligent bus driver has lost control of a bus in which 30 high school teenagers lose their lives. How much more crucial it is to watch for the safety of one's soul!

Are you prepared? Is your soul in readiness for the coming of the Son of Man? And when he appears, what will the verdict on your life be?

Imagine 2:00 o'clock last Friday has come—and gone. You are now in the presence of God. What might be said about you two days after your passing?

In one seminary class, the professor had each student write his own obituary, then lie on a bed with a handkerchief over his face and listen to other members of the class discuss him and his life. The real question, however, is not what your friends might say about you, but what God will say. Are you ready?

Our Lord says, "No one knows about that day or hour ... For in the days before the flood, people were eating and drinking, marrying and giving in marriage, up to the day Noah entered the ark; and they knew nothing about what would happen until the flood came and took them all away. That is how it will be at the coming of the Son of Man" (vv. 36, 38–39).

"Therefore keep watch ..."

Our Spirit of Preparation

A Christian pastor is always to preach "as a dying person to dying people." However, we children of God are not on the brink of falling into hell. You and I, as baptized, redeemed Christians, live in grace, in the mercy and love and care of God. Because of Christ's death on the cross for our sins, we are forgiven people—forgiven even for our sloth and unpreparedness. And so again we exult in the Gradual for this day: "Rejoice greatly, O daughter of Zion! Shout, daughter of Jerusalem! See, your King comes to you, righteous and having salvation."

See ... look ... be prepared. Live in the present tense—each day for itself.

Look back at your life this past week. For most of you, it may have been on a fairly level road—but it could change drastically tomorrow. Some gigantic challenge may meet you within the next day or two—a totally unexpected illness, a calamity in your home or business, a loneliness or desperation the likes of which you have never experienced before in your life. You may meet death itself.

Sickness, calamity, loneliness, desperation, death. Will you be ready?

I submit that your best preparation is to give attention to today. What means most to you in life? What responsibility is primary in your life right now? What is your immediate problem?

Right here and now, trust in God. Cast your cares upon him, for he really cares about you. Fill this present moment with the holy faith which he gives you, with the power which his Holy Spirit alone gives, and prepare for the changes which will surely come, which you cannot foresee but need not fear to see.

In the little things of your life today, prepare for the big emergencies tomorrow. On the ordinary road you travel right now, get ready for the mountain tomorrow. In the green pastures and by the still waters, gird yourself for the valley of the shadow. Immerse yourself in the means of grace—God's Holy Word and Sacraments—and live "in the Lord." Then, when you reach the mountain, the shadow, the emergency, you already will be God-possessed. He will dwell in you already, and you in him. Live by God's grace in the present, and the future will not frighten you.

On a high-school graduation day, one girl gave her classmate the following note: "There are two days which we should not worry about. They are yesterday and tomorrow. All the money in the world cannot bring back yesterday—it has passed forever beyond our control. Tomorrow's sun will rise. Until it does, we have no stake in tomorrow, for it is yet unborn. This leaves one day—today—so let us therefore live it well." (*The Possible Years,* 90)

Sounds nice, doesn't it? But some of it is very bad theology. In the richest Christian sense we do have a stake in tomorrow, especially in the day we will see our Lord face to face. And the sun will rise only if our Lord lets it. But that being granted, when we are living in the Lord, then we can say, "This day will never come again; I will live it to its fullest!"

Living in Hope, Not Fear

Give attention to today in preparation for tomorrow, but do so with hope. Yes, Jesus spoke the biting words of our text, but we need to hear them as a part of his whole teaching, part of the whole of Holy Writ. As we study all that Scripture teaches about preparation for Christ's coming, we see our life of preparation as being one filled not with fear at Christ's coming but with hope. "Perfect love drives out fear" (1 John 4:18). We need not live in anxiety, for our redemption is assured through Christ's death and resurrection. We live in the kind of hope that *knows* we are in the Lord, that we are saved.

With this certainty, we can have an attitude towards life and death quite unlike others around us. Knowing we are going to die, we can live with zest and vividness, because we shall not pass this way again. We can approach life's daily tasks with both satisfaction and detachment—at the same time! Similarly, knowing we are alive, we can live as those who must die but who know Christ will take care of us. He is our source of life now and of life to come. Therefore, we can live and work as if we had 100 years!

Again: How shall we prepare? Listen to the prophet Isaiah: "Seek the LORD while he may be found; call on him while he is near. Let the wicked forsake his way and the evil man his thoughts. Let him turn to the LORD, and he will have mercy on him, and to our God, for he will freely pardon" (Isaiah 55:6-7). Therefore, "Those who hope in the LORD will renew their strength. They will soar on wings like eagles; they will run and not grow weary, they will walk and not be faint" (Isaiah 40:31).

May the words of our Lord in the last days of his ministry ring in your ears: "Come, you who are blessed of my Father; take your inheritance, the kingdom prepared for you since the creation of the world" (Matt. 25:34). He is saying to you, "Earth is not your home; your home is with me. Some day I will call you home. Some day I will usher you to the doorway called death. Be not afraid because I will take you by the hand and lead you through, and you will see me face to face. Until then, you have my peace."

Here is the question you and I have to answer on this Advent Sunday and every day of our life: Are you ready?

By the power of the Holy Spirit you can answer, "Yes, Lord, by your grace I am. Even so, come quickly, Lord Jesus!" Amen.

Are You Standing in the Doorway?
Matthew 3:1-12

I have a question for parents: Did you ever have a child who so misbehaved that in anger you sent the child to the bedroom and said, "Stay in that room until you're sorry enough to come out!" One mother did—and after a few minutes heard her girl's bedroom door creak open and saw the girl in the doorway.

"Are you sorry enough to come out now?" asked the mother.

"No," said the girl, "but I'm sorry enough to want the door left open."

My second question is for everybody here this morning. In your relationship with God, have you come out of the room—the box— you've gotten yourself into? Or are you just standing in the doorway, not quite ready to admit your guilt, depriving yourself of God's forgiveness and full fellowship?

Our text is the familiar account of John the Baptist preaching in the wilderness, calling sinners to repentance. He announced that the kingdom of heaven was at hand, that the Messiah had finally come. So the people came out to John, heard his call, confessed their sins, and were baptized in the River Jordan.

The Pharisees and Sadducees—leaders of the church—also came, but John's message to them was a stern one: "Repentance without fruit is no repentance; Christ's winnowing fork will soon separate the wheat from the chaff, the genuine penitents from the false ones."

John's call is unmistakable; it is a call to genuine repentance. On the basis of John's call, I submit as today's theme that <u>even the most faithful Christian needs repeated repentance—and the blessed fruits that come from God's reaffirmed forgiveness.</u>

Let's consider the implications of this theme in John's call to our own lives today:

    I. The Meaning of Repentance
   II. The Need for Repentance; and
  III. The Goal of Repentance

The Meaning of Repentance

What would you say is the major message to us from Scripture? No, it's not "I suggest that you be good." It's not "keep the Ten Commandments." It's not "do unto others as you would have them do unto you." And it's not "God is love" or "love your neighbor," either.

No, the central challenge of the Scripture to us, in both Old and New Testaments, is "Repent for the forgiveness of sins." It was the clarion call of all the prophets before Christ came. It is the heart of John's message as recorded by Luke (3:3). It was the keynote of our Lord's ministry, as Matthew 4:17 says, "Jesus began to preach, 'Repent, for the kingdom of heaven is near.' "

Later, our Lord called the Twelve together and charged them with the specifics of their mission. And Mark 6:12 records, "They went out and preached that people should repent."

And at the very end of his ministry, just before his ascension, our Lord summed up the Old Testament prophesies as a climactic charge to his disciples, "Repentance to the forgiveness of sins will be preached in his name to all nations" (Luke 24:47, author's translation from better manuscripts), and that the disciples were to be "witnesses of these things" (v. 48). What things? Repentance that leads *to* forgiveness. That is the heart of the biblical message, and that I proclaim to you today.

Repentance! Do you have as difficult a time as I do, grappling with genuine repentance, especially when we hear about it so many times and go through it again and again in our Christian lives? Do you become weary of the treadmill of repenting and repenting and repenting—especially after you've been a Christian for many years? Do you get sick of hearing sermons on it, having it analyzed, having it urged upon you, especially when you have tried by God's grace to live a better Christian life, have made some progress, fallen flat on your face, and wearied of getting up to start all over again?

Each of us here stands in a little different position with respect to John the Baptist's—and our Lord's—call. Some of us are bored with hearing the call again. Others don't want to hear it at all. Others are sick of themselves and welcome the call and the reality about themselves which it brings—God's merciful forgiveness.

In whatever state you are this morning, one thing is clear for each of us: God calls all of us to repentance again this Advent season, this day, this hour. He stands ready to lead us out of the room—the box of sin—we're in, through the doorway, and into the room of his love.

Repentance, though, is more than feeling bad about sin. It is a changing of mind, a complete turning around and away from your sin. True repentance involves contrition, confession, and conversion. Contrition, from the Latin *contritio,* means true sorrow over sin, not *attritio,* just fear of punishment. It means you're more than sorry enough to want just the door left open. You're truly sorry enough to confess and, because of God's forgiveness, to convert (i.e., to change). Repentance is a sense of sin, sorrow over sin, and severance from sin. It's realization you have sinned, regret that you have sinned, and resolution not to sin again—all by the power and grace of God's forgiveness.

Are you ready to repent—to take all three steps?

The Need for Repentance

John's words here were directed with particular severity to those hypocritical religious leaders of the day who also came out to hear him. He made clear that their claim of Abraham as their father—in effect, their status of being kingpins in the kingdom—was irrelevant. The most faithful church member—no matter how long in the church—needs God's repeated call to repentance. This is not just a call to those outside the church or to people living notoriously wicked and evil lives. No, its call is to you and to me.

Some years ago a student at the University of Michigan who flunked his exams was afraid to go home to his family—so he hid in the bell tower of the local Methodist church. Well, there were some strange goings-on in that building for a while. The spaghetti even disappeared from the refrigerator after the Ladies' Aid meeting. No one could figure out what was happening—until they discovered "the man hiding in the church." (*The Possible Years,* 83)

Are you the man—the woman—hiding in the church, hiding behind your membership, assuming you have no need for serious repentance?

There's a big difference, you know, between having "made your confirmation" (that's about all some people did—they "made it") and reliving your baptismal vow every day. Many people thought their religious education was over when they were confirmed, as if their spiritual bags were now packed for the rest of their lives. How many fell away from an active participation within a few years of their confirmation day?

There's a big difference between going to church and being the church, between "saying the creed" and doing the Christian deed. There's a big difference between just going to Communion and receiving the Lord's Supper with a penitent heart and with a joyful spirit that gives thanks for sins forgiven.

Yes, in many ways we just go through the motions—and make our Lord's words apply to us, "These people honor me with their lips, but their hearts are far from me" (Mark 7:6).

Are you, empowered by the Holy Spirit, willing to act now and respond to God's call to repent? Or will you yield to the temptation to procrastinate and say "I'll wait a little longer"? The dying thief on the cross is no model to follow. To paraphrase St. Augustine, "There is but one case of deathbed repentance recorded—the penitent thief—that no one should despair; but there is only one case, so that no one should dare to presume on God."

No, the time for church members to repent is the same time as for everyone: Now. The kingdom of heaven is at hand, said John and Jesus. "Now is the day of salvation," St. Paul reminds us (2 Cor. 6:2). True, you might not die tonight, but why miss out today on the joy of living with Jesus' forgiveness and peace?

The Goal of Repentance

That last comment leads us again to the goal of repentance: Christ working his forgiveness in us.

A famous English surgeon, before anesthetics were invented, gave wise counsel to one of his patients, "Take a long, last look at your hideous death-working sore; then fix your eyes on me and do not take them off till I am done." That's when the healing begins. (Source unknown.)

That's what Christ also says to you today, "Take a long, last look at your hideous death-working sore; then fix your eyes on me, and do not take them off till I am done." That is the ultimate purpose of John's—and our Lord's—call: not hurt, but healing; not damnation, but deliverance. The biblical message is not only Law, but

Gospel. It's not only judgment, but mercy. The Baptist's and our Lord's call is not to fear but to peace: the forgiveness of sins.

Back at the seminary in preaching class we used to ask students the following question. How would you answer it?

"The foremost purpose of preaching the Law to people is that they (a) recognize God's dissatisfaction with their behavior; (b) sense your sympathy with their difficulties; (c) in their minds request you to speak the Gospel help, which they need; (d) find something concrete in the sermon."

And now—the envelope, please.

The right answer is (c): "In their minds request you to speak the Gospel help, which they need."

To be sure, the immediate purpose of the Baptist's call is to make us realize our condition—but towards God's gracious purpose that we repent and receive his gracious forgiveness. The ultimate purpose of God's Law is not to damn us but to make us desire the Good News of the Gospel. Note John's words again: "Repent, for the kingdom of heaven is near."

This is good news, not bad. You are in God's grace now through Christ's death, resurrection, and ascension. Now you are receiving the blessed fruits of Christ's atonement through your Baptism and the means of grace.

And so now you can live with joy, knowing this is your assurance.

Summary

The most faithful Christian among us knows he/she needs this call to repentance. For we all have the Old Adam inside us, and our sinful nature will try to tear down the "new creation" within us until the day we die. As the Introit psalm warns, "He promises peace to his people, his saints—but let them not return to folly."

In declaring John's and our Lord's call to repentance to you again this morning I do not mean to intimate you are all a few short steps away from being eternally damned sinners.

Having truly made confession, as we did again in the liturgy today, we once more hear the joyful news that we are still God's children, still in his family. Our text speaks of those who did repent, "confessing their sins" (v. 6). Therefore, our paean of praise can ring out again: "What a wonderful God we have!"

Christmas is just around the corner. Joy and anticipation fill the air. But that Babe in a crib came to die on a cross. So Advent is a time of repentance as well as rejoicing.

Christmas is coming. But before it comes into your heart and mine this year, we are to answer the voice which is calling to you and me today. If we are very quiet, we will hear Jesus calling to us, standing in the doorway of the room—the box—of our sin, "Sinner, repent," because "whoever comes to me I will never drive away" (John 6:37).

What will your answer be? Will it be the simple words of the penitent, "Jesus, be merciful to me, a sinner"? Then rest assured again this day that the Lord says to you personally, "Your sins are forgiven. Go in peace!"

The Wounded Healer Returns to Restore Us
Hosea 5:15–6:2

Whatever you think of General Douglas MacArthur, his words will endure, "I shall return!" He did, and U.S. Troops were victorious in World War II in the Pacific.

"I shall return!" God also made that promise—even though at times you may feel he won't. In fact, God seems to say that in our text. "I will go back to my place," that is, "I will leave you." But then he adds, "… until they admit their guilt" (Hos. 5:15).

Is there anything—anything at all—about which you feel guilty today? Is there anything in your life for which you have failed to fully and truly repent? Have you ever felt that God has left you? Have you blamed God for your misery and not sought him earnestly in your prayers? In your self-absorption, have you instead withdrawn into yourself and found even more self-pity and emptiness there, rather than returning to God and focusing on him as the only source of peace and joy?

Hosea teaches us that, [theme] <u>when in self-indulgence we refuse to acknowledge God, God leaves us, and we are in misery. Yet though God wounds and tests, he will heal.</u> The focus is God's suffering love. So we are to seek him earnestly and return to him, and he will restore us to life in his presence.

God wounds but heals; he leaves but returns. This is the theme we will consider on this Sunday in Advent. As you know, Advent— "coming"—is the preparatory season before Christmas. Our readiness, watchfulness, and anticipation mark these days. We re-examine ourselves and see our need to repent—even at Christmas time because this Christ Child, who would soon come to be born in a crib, would also die on a cross—*for us.* That's why God's message through Hosea is so important to us today: God wounds but heals; he leaves but returns.

Unfaithfulness

Do you know of a marriage where the husband or wife had really "slept around" a lot, but there was reconciliation, and one spouse forgave the other and took the unfaithful person back? That's what happened to Hosea. His wife committed adultery, and he divorced her; but God asked Hosea to take her back—and he did (chapters 1–3).

That's the scene in the book of Hosea. The account, however, is really a parallel to the marriage between profligate Israel and her God. Because of her spiritual adultery, Yahweh says he is like a lion, a devourer (5:14): "I'll destroy them and go back to my den and see how they respond." The tragedy is that Israel glibly touts the words of 6:1–3, "Come, let us return … he will heal us … After two days he will revive us … as surely as the sun rises, he will appear." The people know the right words, but they admit no real guilt. Their response—like ours—often involves only a shallow repentance. It is like the morning dew that disappears (6:4).

Has your repentance ever been like that? "God seems to be mad at me again. He's gone; but, oh well. He'll be back again soon." If so, God grieves. He wants true repentance, not false promises. "I want more than pious words [6:6]; I want you and me to be together again"—as in a reconciled marriage. He's like a spouse who painfully yearns to get the unfaithful mate to come back. God is a God of suffering love.

Or doesn't the shoe fit? Even though you may not have been guilty of adultery or fornication, are there no ways in which you have taken your sin—and God's suffering love—lightly?

One of the deadliest misconceptions that you and I can fall prey to is to believe that if we aren't gross sinners, we aren't really very sinful at all. For example, when I say the word "immorality," what do you think of? Adultery? Fornication? It means far more than that. As the famous writer Dorothy Sayers has said:

> Perhaps the bitterest commentary on the way in which Christian doctrine has been taught in the last few centuries is the fact that to the majority of people the word immorality has come to mean one thing and one thing only … . A man may be greedy and selfish; spiteful, cruel, jealous, and unjust; violent and brutal; grasping, unscrupulous, and a liar; stubborn and arrogant; stupid, morose, and dead to every noble instinct—and still we are ready to say of him that he is not an immoral man. I am reminded of a young man who once said to me with perfect simplicity, "I did not know there were seven deadly sins; please tell me the names of the other six." (*The Whimsical Christian* [New York: Macmillan, 1987])

You and I are not on the brink of hell this morning. In the Trinitarian invocation at the beginning of the service, we again recalled the Sacrament of Holy Baptism. We are baptized Christians, people in God's grace. But we are still sinful. "There is not a righteous man on earth who does what is right and never sins" (Eccl. 7:20). "Whoever keeps the whole law and yet stumbles at just one point is guilty of breaking all of it" (James 2:10). Therefore, we need God's forgiveness and mercy every day. Without it, we *would* be on the brink of hell.

Rationalization

Think of the sin in your life. We, like the children of Israel, often take it too lightly. We don't really admit it—or we rationalize it, justify it, by blaming the situation, other people, or even God.

When have you blamed the situation? When were you like the person who, when caught in a sin, angrily burst out, "Don't read me lectures! I'm doing the best I can, given the circumstances!" That's a simple determinism which says, "I'm a pawn of forces beyond my control; I'm not really responsible for what I do."

When do you blame other people for your sin? "If she hadn't done that to me, I wouldn't have lashed back by doing what I did." Subtly you seek to shift the blame to the other person. That too is rationalization, self-justification.

When have you blamed God for what happened? "Where were you when I needed you, God? You weren't around when I was tempted, so I went ahead and did it." But that's a lie. God has promised, "No temptation has seized you except what is common to man. And God is faithful; he will not let you be tempted beyond what you can bear. But when you are tempted, he will also provide a way out so that you stand up under it" (1 Cor. 10:13). God never permits Satan, your flesh, or the world to test you beyond your God-given strength to be able to resist.

Even if we have many years in the faith, you and I are guilty. When we are honest with ourselves, we admit that we are self-serving sinners. Satan never sleeps; he seeks to woo even the most faithful Christian into false self-security and attacks us where we are weakest. That is why God tears us, injures us, wounds us (Hos. 6:1)—not to punish us but to reprimand us. The purpose of his Law is not to condemn us but to make us realize our sin and our need to return to him. At times he does return to his place (5:15)—but only until we are humbled and repent. Through our afflictions we are brought back to him (assuming our repentance is not a sham that passes away like the morning dew [6:4]).

As each of us looks at our lives this morning, we must honestly say, "Against you, you only, have I sinned" (Ps. 51:4).

Repentance and Forgiveness

Then comes the blessed result of true repentance. The wounded healer, he who suffered for us on the cross, took on himself these sins of rationalization and blaming others, and now he returns, revives, and restores us, and we live in his presence. Truly, "he was pierced for our transgressions, he was crushed for our iniquities; the punishment that brought us peace was upon him, and by his wounds we are healed" (Is. 53:5).

You and I, praise God, are forgiven people! Forgiven and restored by the shed blood of Jesus Christ, we are back in God's presence again (Hos. 6:2). Although those words (Hos. 6:1–3) were spoken by Israel without sincerity, they were the right words. In Jesus, the wounded healer *has* returned to restore us. And we have the blessing of his presence. Therefore, we say with the psalmist, "I love the house where you live, O LORD, the place where your glory dwells" (Ps. 26:8). No matter what burdens we bring to Christ, we pray, "O Lord, it's good to be back in your presence again. Thank you for returning to me. I took your grace too lightly. It was not an easy forgiveness that your Son won for me by his bitter sufferings and death. Thank you, Lord, for even though I wounded you with my sin, you have returned to me and healed me."

But the story isn't over yet.

Two Lives to Live

A pastor recounts driving through Nevada with his family and stopping for lunch. Nearby, a woman was playing a slot machine. Her husband wanted to leave, but she wanted to stay. "Might as well try again," she said. "You only live once."

About a week later that same pastor was visiting an 86-year-old lady whose left leg recently had been amputated above the knee—a "saint on earth." Her bedroom was a "cathedral of prayer." That day, as the pastor prepared to leave, she said simply, "Pastor, isn't it wonderful that this is not the only life we have?" (*You Say You're Depressed?* 108)

What a contrast in those two statements! To be sure, we have eternal life right now, but life in heaven will be so different that it's like a whole new life to come.

What a God! We have joy in his presence now, and we have it forever in the life ahead. And what a second life to look forward to! As Scripture promises, "He will wipe away every tear from [your] eyes. There will be no more death or mourning or crying or pain" (Rev. 21:4). For all things will become new. Isn't it wonderful that this isn't the only life we have!

Imagine this scene: A person has just arrived at the portals of heaven. A voice asks, "What is the password? Speak it, and you may enter."

"The password?" the person replies tremulously. "Well, is it 'Whoever calls on the name of the Lord shall be saved'?"

"No," replies the voice.

" 'Come, let us return to the Lord'?"

"No."

" 'For God so loved the world that he gave …'?"

"Those are all true sayings," says the voice, "but they are not the password for which I listen today."

"Well, then, I give up," says the person.

And the voice says, "That's it! Come right in!"

You and I are saved by grace alone! May God the Holy Spirit move you again to rejoice in the presence of God here this morning. Hear him say as he said to Israel through Hosea, "I will heal their waywardness and love them freely, for my anger has turned away from them. I will be like the dew to Israel; he will blossom like a lily" (Hos. 14:4-5).

Tomorrow We'll Be There
Isaiah 9:6

 Backward, turn backward, O Time, in your flight;
Make me a child again just for tonight!
(Elizabeth Akers Allen, *Rock Me to Sleep*)

Christmas Eve! How long we have waited for it! And now it is finally here!

In the midst of all the excitement of this night, all the distractions and bedlam of preparation, what is God saying to you and to me? What have we really been getting ready for?

Our text from Isaiah answers with the familiar words, "For to us a Child is born, to us a Son is given," words that stir our hearts mightily with the music of Handel's *Messiah.* When the Holy Spirit inspired these words, the people of Israel were still waiting for the coming of the Messiah. They thought his appearance was imminent, but they still had a long wait ahead of them.

Imagine a company of hikers approaching the mountains. One of them looks at the snow on the mountain range ahead and expects to be there tomorrow. But they are on foot, and the group does not reach the snow the next day. There are many foothills yet to cross.

Christ the Messiah came, but not as soon as the people of Israel thought. Much of history had yet to transpire. But the promise was there; the "Wonderful Counselor, Mighty God, Everlasting Father, Prince of Peace" would come. And he finally did—in the person of Jesus.

You and I here tonight say, "It's Christmas Eve! We're almost there! The shopping is done; the house is ready; the tree is trimmed; the kids are expectant." The coming of the Savior of the world is very real to us tonight. So it should be, for we are now the children of God, and through our Baptism we are now in God's kingdom of grace. On the other hand, the reality of Christmas does not make much difference to us until Christ is born in our hearts.

This, then, is my theme: <u>Because of the darkness in our hearts, he needs to be reborn in our lives every day.</u>

Darkness or Light?

Is your heart, this night, filled with the Light of the world? Or is it still covered with darkness?

A "Small Society" cartoon (Dec. 21–22, 1968) depicts a man and woman walking outside on a starry Christmas Eve. "Beautiful night," he comments. "Yes, it is," she replies. "What would you like for Christmas?" he asks. They walk on a moment. "Peace on earth," she replies. "Peace on earth!" he says incredulously. "Peace on earth," she replies. They walk on again. After some silence he says, "Be serious now, Shirl; what would you really like for Christmas?"

Many people still really don't know or don't want peace this Christmas Eve. As Dr. O. P. Kretzmann once wrote, "I cannot know whether you will be any closer to peace on earth (even a year from now) … Even then when Christmas comes, you will have to guard against measuring heaven by the standards of earth … Peace, even among nations, is not a matter of treaties and guns and atomic bombs … It is a matter of the heart resting in quiet at the manger … There can be no peace in the hearts of men, because no nation can be greater than the men and women who make it." (*Campus Commentary*, Valparaiso University, Valparaiso, Indiana, Christmas, 1967)

We, like the man in the cartoon, may not take seriously the absence of peace throughout the earth. Living in our fairly secure little worlds we can shut out the tragedies of distant wars—or the lack of peace in our own neighborhoods. And to live without that care is to be in darkness—spiritual darkness in which Christ the Light of the world does not shine.

The darkness in our lives can be our frequent living for ourselves to the exclusion of the needs of others. Or, particularly with the dither and bustle of all the Christmas preparation, our lives can be darkened by impatience, bickering, or rough words that are far from the peaceful and gentle spirit Christ wants us to have.

For example, one home on Christmas Eve included a lot of noise and activity. The father was busy with all sorts of packages and last-minute chores. The mother's frayed nerves had reached the breaking point several times. Their one small daughter was constantly in the way no matter what she did. Finally, the girl was simply sent off to bed with harsh words and a hasty "Good night!"

As she prayed alone the Lord's Prayer before going to sleep, all the high-pitched tension of the day took its toll. When she came to the middle of the prayer, she said, "And forgive us our Christmases, as we forgive those who Christmas against us." (Author unknown.)

"Forgive us our Christmases!" How often we need to pray that—because we don't really care enough about making peace for others in the world or even in our own homes. Often there is no real peace in our hearts because we have not really wanted Christ to come to dispel the darkness in our hearts. Instead we have often wanted to remain in the dark, as if Christ had never been born. For that we need to repent. And because of that Christ needs to be reborn in our lives every day.

That's particularly hard at Christmas time, isn't it?—with all the distractions and deceptions of the world around us.

A Theological Affair

A Christmas window of one of the largest department stores in San Francisco had the following words: "What is Christmas? Christmas is wide-eyed children, fairy-land magic, age-old music, and good will in the hearts of men."

Is that all there is?

Two women stopped in front of another store window at Christmas time. In the midst of all the merchandise was a small little Nativity scene. One woman remarked to the other, "What do you know about that! Even the church is trying to horn in on Christmas time."

That comment is similar to another woman's attitude. "Most of the Christmas songs," she complained, "are too distressingly theological!" (From an unpublished manuscript by Robert K. Menzel.)

Well, after all, Christmas was a rather theological affair, wasn't it?

Would that the world could see how theological it really is! Would that we and the rest of the world could stop in our Christmas-shopping traffic jams long enough to see why he came: to bring light into our darkness, hope into our meaninglessness, comfort to our suffering hearts, and true peace to our world and to our homes.

That is what he did for Israel. The first words of this chapter of Isaiah refer to the previous chapter, when everything looked black and melancholy for God's people. But then God came to his people.

The Good News is that for your darkness and mine, in the worst of times, God comes to us too. We have the Light of the world to comfort us, to overcome our troubles. Even as the people of Israel were to comfort themselves with hope on every cloudy and dark day, so you and I are to comfort ourselves in time of trouble with the certainty of Christ's presence.

God's promise is with us: "For to us a Child is born, to us a Son is given, and the government will be on his shoulders. And he will be called Wonderful Counselor, Mighty God, Everlasting Father, Prince of Peace."

He is "*Wonderful* Counselor"—wonderful in his birth, life, death, resurrection, and ascension for us. By God's grace he "forgives us our Christmases" of bickering and self-centeredness. Because of Christ's death for your sins and mine, we *do* have peace this night in our hearts and in our homes. We are a forgiven people, for God is a wonderful God of forgiveness.

And he is a "Wonderful *Counselor.*" He guides you and me in every step of life.

He is the "Mighty God." He always follows through. God always keeps his promises; he never lets you down.

He is "Everlasting Father." Christ, one with God, reigns forever. He is your tender, caring parent through all eternity.

He is "Prince of Peace." With Christ in your heart, you have true peace, for he is the author of peace, the giver of all that is good in your life, now and in that bliss which is to come.

This, then, is our Christmas joy. We who have been in darkness have seen a great light. Therefore, we rejoice, not as those who have no hope, no peace, no light, but as those who have seen the salvation of the world—in a Babe born in a manger.

So What?

And what can we do about this Christmas message?

I suggest a hearty, fun-filled Christmas celebration. This year keep singing those carols! Keep the decorations up! Don't take down that tree! Keep the Christ Child at the heart of everything you do throughout the 12 days of Christmas (until Epiphany). "For to us a Child is born, to us a Son is given, and the government will be on his shoulders. And he will be called Wonderful Counselor, Mighty God, Everlasting Father, Prince of Peace!"

Christmas—As a Little Child
Luke 2:1–20

In the book *Mrs. Miniver* (which was also made into a movie), the author described her family's Christmas, "However much one groaned about it beforehand, however much one hated making arrangements and doing up parcels and ordering several days' meals in advance—when it actually happened, Christmas Day was always fun." (Quoted in an unpublished sermon by Robert K. Menzel.)

Tomorrow, though, may be the big let-down. In fact, it's already come for some. On Christmas Eve in one grocery store the woman at the bakery counter was methodically tearing down all the festive decorations—at 3:15 in the afternoon! Another clerk said to a customer, "I had so hoped they'd leave the decorations up at least until New Year's." Yes, the world's so-called Christmas is soon over. Much of what we saw and heard was all for effect, the effect of buying and selling, of giving to be getting. (Comment heard by the author.)

How will you properly celebrate this blessed Christmas Day—and the joyous days that are to come in its aftermath? I submit there is only one way to celebrate Christmas: "As a little child."

Our text is the well-beloved Christmas Gospel. In it, one point is repeated several times: a *baby*—a *son*—a *child*. God in his majesty and might could have chosen to dazzle us with his omnipotent power in some spectacular fashion. Instead he chose to reveal himself as a lowly babe in a manger.

Therefore, our theme is: <u>Only when a child came was there a Christmas; and only as you become a child can you have and keep Christmas.</u> We examine the meaning and deeper implication of that by seeing how we are to:

    I. Learn from the Child;

    II. Learn as a child; and

    III. Witness to the Child

Learn from the Child

First of all, we are to be ready to listen when God speaks, even when his message to us doesn't come in the way we expect it. Sometimes, "a little child shall lead them." A child told a military captain that he could be healed of his leprosy. A child was called to our Lord's knee to show the stature one had to have to enter the door of his kingdom. A child brought the bread and fish which our Lord used to feed the multitude. And in these latter days God revealed himself to us through a Son—a child, Christ the Lord—who fulfilled the promise made in the Old Testament, "To us a Child is born, to us a Son is given" (Is. 9:6).

When we see this Babe "wrapped in swaddling clothes, lying in a manger" (Luke 2:12 KJV), we are tempted to forget that he is the Almighty God. But when we hear a heavenly host of angels proclaiming him to be so, then the Spirit moves us to confess, "Surely it can be no other than the Son of God!"

But many people are not ready to receive God "as a little child." Many people on that first Christmas night were not. Camped around Jerusalem were the Roman legions, none of whom could be accused of being child-like. It was Christmas Day there too, but it was only for the shepherds on the Judean hills that the angels sang. It was Christmas Day in Herod's palace, but the Savior was born in a lowly stable and to a humble maiden named Mary. In Athens were the wise men of Greece, but they saw no star. It appeared to others: Wise men who longed to see the Light of the world.

Learn as a Child

Are you ready for Christmas? Ready to get down on your knees before the manger, ready to stoop down to the level of a child so you can have the proper perspective from which alone you can see this miracle in a manger?

In a playground in Chicago, small children enter a "tiny tot play lot" through a low gateway shaped like a keyhole. Admittance to this playground depends on the ability of the child to walk upright through the low gate. In other words, their size is their ticket.

Your size, too—the size of your ego—determines whether or not you can have Christmas and the kingdom of heaven this lowly

Baby would bring you. "Remember this!" Jesus said. "Whoever does not receive the Kingdom of God like a child will never enter it" (Luke 18:17 TEV). This is the only way.

We need the simplicity and trust of a child-like faith to say, "I am a sinner. I daily fall short of what God expects of me. I don't deserve God's mercy and forgiveness. But I have a Savior. I can't understand all the mystery and wonder of Christmas—how God's salvation can come this way. But I can believe it. This baby, Jesus, is my Savior from sin and the Savior of the whole world.

"I do need a Savior for the sin that besets me. Forgive me, Lord, for often devising a god of my own liking and wanting my life on my own terms. Forgive me for the times I have doubted your love for me. Forgive me for not trusting that you know what is best for me.

"Now, in child-like faith, O Lord, I ask your forgiveness. I come in penitent, trusting faith in this Christ-child as my Savior."

What burdens your heart this day? What fear or sorrow keeps you from the great joy about which the angels sang? Again, let us learn from a little child. Our teacher is a 6-year-old girl named Becky.

Becky's home life gave little to be joyful about. Her father, an alcoholic, spent little time at home; and when he was there, he and her mother spent much of their time yelling at each other. Becky would run to hide in her bedroom for hours.

Becky liked Sunday school, though—especially practice for the children's Christmas program. She was a sheep; no speaking part—not for quiet, introverted Becky.

One Sunday, when practice in the auditorium was over and the children had returned to their Sunday school rooms, Becky's teacher found her still in the auditorium, sitting on the floor next to the manger. She had taken the Jesus doll out of the manger and was holding it tightly in her arms. She was singing "Jesus Loves Me."

Becky had found a moment of great joy amid the pain in her life. The answer to our failures and imperfections, too, is found in the perfection of Jesus Christ, the source of our celebration. (Adapted from Myles Schultz, in *Seasonal Illustrations,* 18–19)

Do you still have a child-like faith such as this? Can you this blessed Christmas Day still come as a child to see the child in the manger? To rephrase Jesus' words, "Whoever receives the kingdom of God like a child *will* enter it."

Witness to the Child

By the Holy Spirit's power, those who have the faith of a child in the Child of Bethlehem want to witness to the Child. "When [the shepherds] had seen him, they spread the word concerning what had been told them about this child" (v. 17). Do you, no matter how many Christmases you have celebrated, still follow the child-like example of the shepherds in our text and tell those with whom you work and live about this child?

A little girl was about to undergo a dangerous operation. Just before the doctor administered the anesthetic, he said to her, "Before we can make you well, we must put you to sleep." The girl responded, "Oh, if you are going to put me to sleep, then I must say my prayers first." She folded her hands, closed her eyes, and said, "Now I lay me down to sleep, I pray the Lord my soul to keep. If I should die before I wake, I pray the Lord my soul to take. And this I ask for Jesus' sake. Amen." Later on the surgeon admitted that he prayed that night for the first time in 30 years. (*Three Thousand Illustrations,* 103)

Summary

Only as you witness to this child with the unabashed simplicity of faith of the "little ones" of the kingdom of God can you celebrate Christmas. This very day, in David's town, your Savior is born—Christ the Lord!

So come again—as you have ever since you were a child, ever since you were baptized—and enfold this Babe in the manger of your faith. Give yourself as the shepherds did to him because he gave himself on the cross for your sins and paid for your eternity in the bosom of the Father. By the power of the Holy Spirit make a Christmas gift of yourself as you tell others how Christmas is fulfilled in your eternal salvation through this wondrous Child.

Luther comments on the shepherds in one of his Christmas sermons, "This is wrong. We should correct this passage to read, 'They went and shaved their heads, fasted, told their rosaries, and put on cowls.' Instead we read, 'The shepherds returned.' Where to? To their sheep." (Roland H. Bainton, translator and arranger, *The*

Martin Luther Christmas Book [Philadelphia: Muhlenberg Press, 1948], 50) The sheep would have been in a sorry way if they had not.

You here this day: Go back to your homes, to your neighbors, to your jobs. The sheep are waiting for you. Tell them of the Christ-child who was born a Savior *for them.*

And as you leave today through our church doors smaller in stature but greater in faith than when you came in, I say to you, "A very blessed Christmas—in the name of the Christ Child."

The Twelfth or the First Day of Christmas?
1 Corinthians 9:22

[The following is adapted from a sermon preached at the Missions and Communication Congress, Concordia Theological Seminary, Fort Wayne, Indiana, October 11, 1990.]

A little boy and his father were out on a walk when they noticed a gathering of people around a large clearing.

"Look, Dad," said the boy. "They're throwing all their old Christmas trees on a big pile and burning them."

They could hear the group singing "On the twelfth day of Christmas." The group became quiet as a leader read a prayer. "O God, by the leading of a star you once made known to all nations your only-begotten Son; now lead us, who know you by faith, to know in heaven the fullness of your divine goodness …"

"What's going on, Dad?" said the boy.

"Today is Epiphany," the father explained, "twelve days after Christmas. These people are celebrating the original first Christmas day, the most ancient celebration of Christmas in Christendom." And he went on to explain the tradition.

Did you know that? We think of today as the twelfth day of Christmas, but it actually is the first Christmas day—and is so celebrated in many Christian traditions, the Orthodox Church, for example. Jesus' birth originally was celebrated on January 6th, but the western church moved the festival to December 25th in order to compete with the pagan festival of Saturnalia. Still, though, we remember January 6th, Epiphany, as the revelation of Jesus to the Gentiles.

Epiphany comes from the two Greek words *epi* and *phaino,* "to show forth" or "appear." Our Lord's glory shone forth on this day, and he was worshiped by the Magi, the Wise Men. The significance of that visit and of Epiphany is that Christ's coming was not only for the Jewish people, but for all people. As the collect says, "You once made known *to all nations* your only-begotten Son."

So, on Epiphany we recall the awesomeness of the nativity of our Lord, the revelation of God in the person of Jesus. "God was reconciling the world to himself in Christ, not counting men's sins against them. And he has committed to us the message of reconciliation. We are therefore Christ's ambassadors" (2 Cor. 5:19–20).

We recall that Christ was born in a crib for a purpose: to die on a cross *for us*. And "for us" means *all* the people in the world. That is the major focus of this day in the church year. Because of that, we emphasize on Epiphany and throughout the Epiphany season Christ's Great Commission to witness to all nations, including especially the people in our own backyards. I want to focus on our Lord's own way of witnessing: becoming, in the Apostle Paul's words, "all things to all men" (1 Cor. 9:22)—a prototype of the way we too can witness.

As a way to focus on Jesus' methods of witnessing about himself, I will be paraphrasing Richard Lischer in his book *Speaking of Jesus: Finding the Words for Witness*. (Fortress Press, 1982, reprinted by Concordia Seminary Press, Fort Wayne, Indiana) Note that Christ and his method of communicating is not just "an example to follow." For [theme] <u>we often fail in our feeble attempts at witnessing. But throwing ourselves on the mercy of Christ, we receive forgiveness. And he does that in us which we are unable to do.</u>

So, ask yourself, What does our Lord teach about his own method of communicating the Good News of the Gospel?

Dialogic

First of all, our Lord's communication was dialogic. He was an active listener, and he entered fully into the thought world of the person with whom he was speaking. He didn't use the questions of his dialog partners as springboards for his own premeditated answers. Rather he built on that other person's questions as a way of probing that person's heart.

A man came to him and said, "Good Teacher." But Jesus soon responded, "Why do you call me good?" (Mark 10:17–18). "Do you want to inherit eternal life? Why? How badly?" Jesus got directly to the man's motives and priorities. Through dialog the man participated in examining his motives; and as Mark tells us, he "went away sad, because he had great wealth" (v. 22).

One other very brief yet poignant element should be noted in this scene. In the face of impending rejection, Jesus shows his tender compassion. It's just one line, but powerful: "Jesus looked at him and loved him" (v. 21). Compassion always is to be the hallmark of our witnessing. Is that true of your witnessing to others?

Holistic

Second, Jesus' way of communicating the Good News was holistic; he approached people as whole beings. He was concerned for the body as well as the soul. He forgave the sick and healed the sinners. Remember the scene with a paralytic? "My son, your sins are forgiven." But then Jesus also added, "Pick up your mat, and go home!" (Mark 2:5, 11 TEV). In Jesus there was never a discrepancy between word and deed.

In the heart of the African jungle a woman on safari was visiting a leper colony. She was very well dressed and looked about her with disdain. The heat was intense; the flies buzzing. Then she noticed a nurse bending down in the dust, tending the open, pus-filled sores of a leper. Drawing herself back, she remarked, "Why, I wouldn't do that for all the money in the world!" To which the nurse quietly replied, "Neither would I." That nurse did not just love with words, but with deeds of love. Her ministry was holistic—as was our Lord's. (*The Best of Your Life,* 91) Do you relate to people as whole persons?

Situational

Third, Jesus' approach in evangelization was situational. He went "on location" with the Gospel. He found Matthew in the tax collector's office, the Samaritan woman at the town well, Zacchaeus up a tree, Mary at the fireplace, Martha in the kitchen. He ate and drank with sinners. He went where the people were: the city bank, the community park, K Mart, and the temple. He reached out to them in their situation-in-life (their *Sitz im Leben*). He didn't wait for them to come to him, like the church member who says, "Well, the people of our town know where our church is. Been here 100 years. Let them come to us."

No, Jesus went to the people, to where they were. Do you witness where you work?

Simple Language

Fourth, Jesus communicated in simple language. Amos Wilder, in his discussion of the parables, speaks of the "secularity" of Jesus' language. Mark tells us "the common people heard him gladly" (12:37 KJV)—probably because they could understand him (Richard Lischer suggests).

At the same time he followed the important communication principle of starting with the known and going to the unknown. Jesus would say, "See how the lilies of the field grow" (Matt. 6:28). And someone would respond, "Why, I know just what you mean, Lord! I was just digging the earth around them this morning!"

Or he would say, "A man was going down from Jerusalem to Jericho, when he fell into the hands of robbers" (Luke 10:30). And someone would respond, "I know just what you're talking about! Why, Uncle Ben got mugged on that same road just last Saturday!"

Jesus spoke the language of the people—so clearly that it resulted in the religious leaders resenting his claim to be God, and thereby finding him deserving of death. Do people understand you when you present the Gospel to them? Do you "speak their language"?

Decisive

And finally, Jesus' approach to Gospel communication was decisive. He called his listeners to a decision, to an ultimate response to who and what he was. "Follow me," he said.

Today we hear much about a "decision for Christ." But that is often only for the moment; discipleship is for the long haul. Whenever decision is separated from discipleship, the result is what Dietrich Bonhoeffer called "cheap grace." Listen to his words in the *Cost of Discipleship:*

> Cheap grace is the grace we bestow on ourselves ... the preaching of forgiveness without requiring repentance, Baptism without church discipline, communion without confession. Cheap grace is grace without discipleship. (R. H. Fuller, translator [New York: The Macmillan Company, 1959], 47)

Jesus moved among people to effect the decisive change known as repentance and the permanent process known as discipleship.

And one final word on the call to a decision to repent. That is the ultimate message of our Lord in connection with his method. "Repent, for the kingdom of heaven is at hand!" That was a blunt challenge to turn from sin that the Good News might be announced!

It is the heart of the message of the Scripture, Old Testament and New. It is the call of the prophets, of John the Baptist; it's the heart of the sermons in the book of Acts; and it is Christ's final climactic words to his disciples (Luke 24:46–48), that they should preach to all nations "repentance *to* [not "and"] the forgiveness of sins" (author's translation from better manuscripts). Then the Good News can be announced, "For God so loved the world that He gave His only begotten Son, that whoever believes in Him should not perish but have everlasting life" (John 3:16 NKJV).

"If anyone is in Christ, he is a new creation; the old has gone, the new has come! All this is from God, who reconciled us to himself through Christ and gave us the ministry of reconciliation: that God was reconciling the world to himself in Christ, not counting men's sins against them. And he has committed to us the message of reconciliation. We are therefore Christ's ambassadors, as though God were making his appeal through us" (2 Cor. 5:17–20).

As we repent for our failed witness, God forgives our feeble efforts through the mercy of Christ.

And that leads to a final truth we are called to embrace as we follow Christ's pattern of communicating the Gospel message: We are saved totally through our Spirit-empowered faith in Jesus Christ, not by any of our own doing.

We have not been speaking just of "virtues" to emulate, of Jesus' wise methods of communication. That is the evil of moralism, which exalts a virtue as a way to achieve spirituality. Biblical Christianity sees virtue as a result of the Gospel, active in the believer's life.

Further, Christ is not just "guide," "model," or "example." He is prototype. For example, we focus not on his humility as a precept to follow, but on his humiliation, his sacrifice for us by which we are forgiven and then called to the fruits of faith, empowered solely by the Holy Spirit (see Gal. 5 and 6). Christ as prototype is the first fruits of those who believe in him. It is Christ in me (see Col. 1:27).

Therefore, today you and I are called to renewed dedication to the Epiphany message to be "all things to all men," that "God may be made known to all nations."

May you, empowered by the Holy Spirit, communicate the Gospel as did our Lord. He was dialogical, holistic, situational, plain in his language, and decisive. Then others, learning of their Savior, will join you and me and the shepherds on that first Christmas night, of whom Luke wrote, "The shepherds returned, glorifying and praising God for all the things they had heard and seen" (2:20).

Are You on a Power Trip?
Matthew 20:26

[Based on Richard Kapfer's fine material in *Lent: A Time for Renewal.*]

What Christian symbols do you have at your home or on your car? A cross or two? A stylized poster of a Bible passage? A fish, the secret recognition sign of the early Christians?

Do you know what we all should have? A picture of a towel and a wash basin. Why? Because they are symbols of humility and servanthood. It's too bad Albrecht Dürer painted praying hands; maybe wet hands would have been better. And maybe we ought to have drills on how to use towels and basins, much like learning CPR. True, humility advertised isn't being humble, but humility is part of being a Christian.

That's what we want to talk about this Ash Wednesday evening. Our specific theme is: <u>Although we are often proud and want to lord it over others, Christ calls us to be humble and to be servants of others, as he humbled himself for us.</u>

Needed: More Towels and Basins

It is Maundy Thursday evening, a few days after the ugly scene when Mrs. Zebedee came to Jesus and asked that her two sons be given positions of honor by Jesus' side in his kingdom. Now they were all in the Upper Room where the Passover was to be celebrated. Since there were only the Twelve plus Jesus, somebody had to take on the servant's role, for their feet had to be washed before eating. Nobody moved. The food was getting cold. The one who moved would be the doormat, the fool, the loser, and he would give up his claim to a leadership position.

Is that what happens in our lives? A couple sits in the pastor's office, all arms folded, looking away from each other, saying nothing. They know that someone has to speak, someone has to give in, but giving in means failure, admission of guilt, humiliation, contempt, and "losing."

Or a woman in the altar guild walks into the chancel and sees the flowers neatly arranged by another member of the congregation. She rearranges the flowers the way *she* would like them. Power. Control.

A group of high school students excludes a lonely classmate from their little in-group. Power. Control.

A person blessed by God with extra money gives a too-large check to someone who has voluntarily helped the individual in some way—not in thanks but to escape feeling indebted and weak. Power and control.

Sad to say, the longer people are in power positions, the more they think that they deserve the position, that there is some great quality within them that others don't have.

Where are you in these pictures? What are the ways in which you lack humility and seek to lord it over other people? Consider the power plays you use in your family, with friends, at school or work—yes, even here in the church. And even if our manipulations are little, they betray a much deeper problem in our hearts: of being self-serving, not serving others.

Our Lord Jesus Christ gives us quite a different picture of our expected role as Christians. Go back to the Upper Room. Every disciple is waiting for someone else to move first toward the basin. Finally someone did move: Jesus. He took towel and basin, knelt down, and began washing feet, one by one. How could Jesus stoop so low? Jesus answered by contrasting the kingdom of the world to the kingdom of heaven. "I have set you an example that you should do as I have done for you. I tell you the truth, no servant is greater than his master, nor is a messenger greater than the one who sent him. Now that you know these things, you will be blessed if you do them" (John 13:15–17).

Our Lord Jesus Christ in this Lenten season calls us not just to contemplate his action of humility but to be like him—"little Christs"—in all areas of our lives. Seeing how far we fall short of being "little Christs," we need to repent often and say with the penitent, "Lord, be merciful to me, a sinner."

Renewal of Servanthood

Lent is a time for renewal. It is a time for a whole new orientation of our hearts. As Peter said to Jesus, "Lord ... not just my feet but my hands and my head as well" (John 13:9). Rather than sing "Take my life and let it be"—period!—we ask instead, "Lord, take my life and renew it by the power of your Holy Spirit. Move my whole being not to be served but to serve."

Tonight Servant Jesus bends down from heaven to earth to forgive us, to wash us clean from sin. The one crowned with thorns comes to crown us as children of the kingdom. The naked one comes to place on us the robes of righteousness. The crucified Christ arises from the grave to free us from the world's deadness and to give us new life and greatness.

What does it mean for your life to wear his crown, to have his robe and life wrapped around you? Are you a parent or a child? In what ways can you, in loving response to the Gospel, serve your parents or child because you are in God's kingdom? Are you single? How can you live as a servant with your friends and serve them? You married couples, what can you do to be subject to each other out of reverence for Christ? Members of this congregation, in what ways can you, by the power of the Holy Spirit and in adoration of our crucified Redeemer, make this church a community of care, a haven from selfishness, a place where people serve one another in love?

Servanthood means repenting, being renewed, and learning that "whoever wants to become great among you" is called to be a servant of Servant Jesus. The power for this renewal comes to us again and again through our Lord, the great servant who still stoops down to serve us, to cleanse us, to pick us up, and to give us power. We receive his service and his strength in our daily searching of the Word, in the power of the Holy Spirit affirming our Baptism, and in receiving the Lord's Supper with a penitent mind and a joyous heart.

May Lent be for you a time for renewal of servanthood. It begins at the cross. Jesus himself will hand you the towel and the basin and point you to where you should go. Most important, he will go with you.

Are You Standing in the Semicircle?

1 Corinthians 10:16–17

I read once of a family that practiced forgiveness around their fireplace each New Year's Eve. They would take down the last year's calendar from the wall, and a page at a time they would remember the events of the past year. January would be torn off first, and with it came memories of a birthday party or some other joyous family event. After a laugh or "Remember that?" January would be laid in the flames. This would be done 11 more times, until the last month's page was put in the fire.

Not all the memories were happy ones. The family members also recalled the times of anger, the misunderstandings, the hurt and pain they had caused one another. But they also recalled the forgiveness that Christ had made possible between them and that they had shared with one another.

That's the kind of forgiveness to practice—daily, but also totally, because God has so forgiven us. And that's the forgiveness of which we are assured in Holy Communion. Our sins are forgiven, indeed *have been* forgiven in the one-for-all and once-for-all act of Jesus' death on Calvary and his resurrection on Easter morn.

Note the words in our text for tonight. Participation is stressed twice: "Is not the cup of thanksgiving for which we give thanks a *participation* in the blood of Christ? And is not the bread that we break a *participation* in the body of Christ?" Participating in his body and blood, we participate in his gracious forgiveness, both as recipients and transmitters of it.

What joy is ours tonight! Observe the atmosphere in the chancel. The note of sorrow that we have heard all Lent is stilled this evening, and the Holy Supper is celebrated with rejoicing. The mood is one of exultation, not gloom. Therefore, our theme: <u>We often miss the full meaning and depth of the Lord's Supper, but God calls us to see and receive the power and blessings of the Supper for our lives.</u>

A Dynamic Drama

Holy Communion is not a dead doctrine but a dynamic drama. It is stirring, moving. It has a cast of characters: God and humanity.

The script for the drama is in the Holy Scriptures. The plot is almost melodramatic. It is the rescue of a fallen child through an amazing plan devised by the divine Father. And this drama is told every time we celebrate Holy Communion.

We are swept with all humanity into the gripping plot as it develops. Each week, as we take our place in the wings of the stage of history and witness the drama of the Lord's institution of his Holy Supper, we see the broad sweep of the dramatic events of salvation pass before our eyes again as together we remember the Lord's death until he comes again.

At least that is what this service of joy and praise is supposed to be. But how often is it that way for you?

Have you ever attended a Holy Communion service and refused to feel thanksgiving in your heart? How often have you sung "Glory be to God on high" like a funeral dirge, with no joy of sins forgiven, with no lifting up of hearts? Has your *Te Deum* been tedium? How can you expect to be spiritually refreshed if you have lost the concept of joyful thanks that the Lord meant for us to share in the blessed Sacrament of his body and blood?

Berthold von Schenk once wrote:

Doubtless this is the cause of much spiritual weakness in our church life. It was not so in the beginning. The central worship of the early church was the Holy Communion. The prime motive which led Christians to form themselves into a fellowship was the desire to worship in their special Christian way. That was the celebration of the Holy Communion. Back of their coming together was, first and foremost, the desire to celebrate the real presence of Christ in the Communion. We have gone a far way from the pristine Church. (*The Presence: An Approach to the Holy Communion* [New York: Ernst Kaufmann, 1945], 23-24)

Or as another author puts it:

This realization of the death of our Lord is a means of an active fellowship with Christ. The believer absolutely yields his person to that transcendent vision of his crucified Redeemer, and thus enters into communion with Christ himself. Christ takes him, penetrates him, and "assimilates him to himself." (Olin Alfred Curtis, *The Christian Faith* [New York: Eaton & Mains, 1905], 432-33)

Do you sense this closeness with Christ as you commune? Do you forget yourself, your record of performing during the week, your deeds, your offerings to God, and instead, at this altar, open yourself up to him and say, "Here, Lord, I am empty; fill me with yourself"?

> Nothing in my hand I bring;
> Simply to thy cross I cling.
> Naked, come to thee for dress;
> Helpless, look to thee for grace;
> Foul, I to the fountain fly;
> Wash me, Savior, or I die.
>
> (*Lutheran Worship* 361:3)

Are These Your Words?

One of the saddest, most misinformed views of the Sacrament is from the person who says, "I don't go to the Lord's Supper unless I've really been improving in my spiritual life, unless I've really cleaned up the things I've done wrong, and have really become worthy of going to communion." This perversion of the meaning of the Sacrament may come from a misunderstanding of the words in the King James Version, "He that eateth and drinketh unworthily, eateth and drinketh damnation to himself" (1 Cor. 11:29). However, those words do not mean that people can make themselves "worthy" to go to the Lord's Supper. Rather, our worthiness comes only from Christ, who gives us the forgiveness of our sins. The words of that passage mean that whoever eats and drinks without being *penitent,* without being *sorry* for one's sins, eats and drinks judgment on oneself. The Lord's Supper is not for the righteous person but for the sinner—and that means everybody in this church tonight!

So it's not what you and I bring to God. Our hands are empty. Instead, God gives us of himself. He gives us the body and the blood of his Son for the forgiveness of our sins.

Therefore, we *participate*—as our text stresses twice.

Standing in the Semicircle

At the same time that we note the intensely personal nature of the Lord's Supper, we also need to grasp the powerful corporate experience involved. Paul points out, "Because there is one loaf, we, who are many, are one body, for we all partake of the one loaf" (1 Cor. 10:17).

Maundy Thursday is a time for renewal of Christian unity. It is a renewal in our common Lord, our common blessings, and our common task.

It is a time for *renewal in our common Lord* so that we can be done with those things that usurp Christ's place within our hearts.

It is a time for *renewal in our common blessings* so that the life of Jesus may be manifested in our mortal bodies (2 Cor. 4:10–11).

It is a time for *renewal in our common task* of confessing our faith, making a unanimous confession of all that Christ has taught (Matt. 28:20).

It is a time to share our joys and sorrows (1 Cor. 12:26). It is a time to stand together against Satan. We will not be such easy prey for Satan when we remain in fellowship with one another. We can better resist Satan when we strengthen our fellowship by partaking of Holy Communion (Acts 2:42). We are not solo Christians. We need each other. Alone, we stumble and fall. United in Christ, we move ahead, empowered by the Holy Spirit to do his will.

A little girl was lost in a large cornfield. It was winter, and the temperature was well below the freezing mark. Rescuers searched for her for hours, but to no avail. Finally, one person suggested that the group start at one end of the field and, holding hands, traverse the field systematically. Finally, they found the child, but she was frozen to death. The father, grief-stricken, cried out, "My God, why didn't we join hands together before?" (*For Example,* 96)

You and I, members of this congregation: Are we always holding hands together in the work our Lord has given us to do? It is a time for renewal of our Christian unity in a common Lord, common blessings, and a common task. Our Lord will do that again in Holy Communion here tonight. Then we will be a body of Christians who together confess Christ, support one another, and stand firm against temptation.

One thing more needs to be said about the corporate nature of Holy Communion. Not only do we share a joy as we commune together with our family, our friends, and our fellow church members, but we also stand in a mystical fellowship with all those of our family and friends who have died "in the Lord"—a fellowship that is heightened at the moment we commune.

Have you ever been in an old rural church with a semicircular communion rail going half way around the altar? Its design is meant to illustrate that the circle of communicants is mystically completed as it continues around the altar and up around the throne of God in heaven at that moment when we chant, "with angels and archangels and with all the company of heaven, 'Holy, holy, holy Lord, God of Sabaoth! Heaven and earth are full of your glory.' "

Just listen! You can hear them singing with you—the angels of heaven, the great saints of ages past, your grandparents or your parents, or the spouse/brother/sister or child who died. At the moment you commune, you are swept together with them into one great host, rejoicing and praising God and saying, "Hosanna in the highest. Blessed is he who comes in the name of the Lord. Hosanna in the highest." They are not dead. They are "with the Lord." And we, united with them, endlessly praise his holy name.

Aware of that circle that extends into heaven and to all eternity, we have joy. It's intensely personal, for you are penetrated by your Savior. It's intensely corporate, for you are bound together with others here and others there in a living, loving Christ.

So. Come, you who are blessed by our heavenly Father! Inherit and feast on the heavenly banquet table prepared for you since the creation of this world (see Luke 22:30).

Are You a "Spectator Christian"?
Romans 3:24–25

[This sermon reflects some of Dr. Gerhard Aho's insights in "An Examination of Renewal in Relation to Faith," *Lent: A Time for Renewal.* Some of my material is to be credited to Edwin C. Munson, *The Cross* (Minneapolis: Augsburg, 1936).]

A pastor in the Pacific Northwest tells of the dramatization of Christ's trial and crucifixion by the youth group at his church. The youth director played the role of Christ, the youth the jeering mob. "Crucify him! Crucify him!" they shouted and then dragged the youth director into the backyard of the church and hung him up on an improvised cross.

The pastor stood to the side of the assembly to see how the drama was going. The youth were hushed as "Christ" hung there and spoke these words to the youth group, "Even though you are doing this to me, I still love you."

Then the pastor noticed an 8-year-old girl standing in the front of the group, transfixed by the scene. He looked at her and saw real tears streaming down her face. "And," the pastor stated later, "I was envious of her. For us professionals it was a performance. For her, it was the real thing."

So often you and I come to a Good Friday service and merely observe what is happening to Christ. We are uninvolved spectators. Yet the Savior of the world is hanging there, suffering and dying for your sins and mine on the cross. (*Lent: A Time for Renewal,* 113)

If you have ever watched a ship go through some locks on its way up a river, you know that it always enters the lock at a low level. The lower gate is then closed, and the water from the upper river is permitted to flow into the lock. The ship rises higher and higher until it is on a level with the river above the dam. Only then can the ship go on with its journey up the river.

What the lock is for the ship, Lent can be for the Christian. Lent receives you at a low spiritual level, but it floods you with such peace and pardon and power that it lifts you up and sends you forth on a higher level in your Christian life. Lent seeks to lift you from where you are to where you should be, from sin to salvation, from spiritual lethargy to spiritual vitality—to a renewed faith.

Our text for tonight capsulizes that faith: "[We] are justified freely by his grace through the redemption that came by Christ Jesus. God presented him as a sacrifice of atonement, through faith in his blood" (Rom. 3:24–25).

As you contemplate the cross this Good Friday, behold this Savior and this salvation. I present him to you with this theme: <u>So that in faith you may more clearly see your Redeemer as he finishes his walk on the Way of Sorrows, may these four elements mark your worship: detachment, decision, self-denial, and devotion.</u>

Detachment

This harried, hurried world of ours sorely needs time for contemplation. Scripture says, "Don't let the world around you squeeze you into its own mould" (Rom. 12:2 JBP), and yet so many of us followers of the Master are letting just that happen in our lives. We live too much for the temporal and the seen, forgetting that it dims our vision of heaven and the goal toward which we run. As Wordsworth said in his poem titled with the first line:

 The world is too much with us;
Late and soon, getting and spending,
We lay waste our powers.

Good Friday invites you to withdraw from the tensions of life for an hour to develop poise and power for the Gethsemanes that lie ahead in your life. Christ prepared for Calvary by secluding himself from the world in order to commune with his heavenly Father. If he needed detachment from the world to prepare for his great ordeal, how much more don't you? This hour is one step toward fulfilling that need in your life.

Albert Schweitzer tells the story of when he first went into the interior of Africa. The caravan was accustomed to stopping at about four or five o'clock each day. But on this particular day, everything suddenly came to a dead halt at about 2:00 P.M. Schweitzer went up ahead to find out what had happened. One of the leaders explained, "The natives have been pushing ahead so fast and are so out of breath that they all said they had to stop and let their souls catch up with their bodies." They were out of breath; for them, breath was the life principle, the soul.

In your life, you may have come a long way. But has your soul caught up with your mind and your body? Good Friday invites you to pause so that they may again be united. (*For Example,* 74)

May your faith tonight bring detachment from the world so that, as our Lord often did in his life, you may "come apart and rest awhile."

But this detachment should have a purpose: a renewed faith in the crucified Christ. That means having more than just knowledge about Christ, about being justified by grace. It means a decision, empowered by the Holy Spirit, to live in the light of that faith.

Decision

During Passion Week, some Greeks approached Philip, saying, "We would like to see Jesus" (John 12:21). Well, they saw him all right—suspended from a cross. I wonder if they realized what was happening as Jesus hung between two thieves. Countless millions around us today do not see there the One who holds in his hands the answer to their eternal life or eternal death.

How vital it is that we Christians, who have by the Holy Spirit decided to *live* our gift of faith in Christ, bring the blessed Gospel to those who by their lives of indifference are daily deciding against the gift itself! Napoleon used to say, "In every battle there is a crisis, 10 or 15 minutes only, on which the outcome depends. To make proper use of this short space of time means victory; its neglect, defeat!"

So it is in your life. A prompt and proper decision often decides a destiny. If you neglect the development of your talents, it can be disastrous. Victory or defeat in your life frequently hangs on the thin thread of a seemingly insignificant opportunity.

So consider the opportunities you may have in your life to tell others about "the redemption that came by Christ Jesus." On this Good Friday night, will you decide, quickened by the Holy Spirit, to speak for Christ more openly, more patiently, more persistently? For

Jesus calls us o'er the tumult
Of our life's wild, restless sea.
Day by day his sweet voice soundeth,
Saying, "Christian, follow me."
(*The Lutheran Hymnal* [hereafter *TLH*] 270)

Self-Denial

Some Christians practice a short-term "discipline" during Lent by eliminating some item from their menu or cutting out some worldly amusement. But true self-denial is more ongoing than that. Just as athletes who want to win train all year long and do not work only during the contest, so Christians need to work on living their faith. They need a lasting commitment to self-denial and self-control, a God-given attitude of mind throughout life that approaches each day's decisions with total dedication to Christ.

How can you expect to resist a great temptation in the future when you yield to small temptations right now, day after day? How can you expect to enjoy the companionships and happiness of heaven if you shun the companionships of Christ's disciples here and seek joy in places and pleasures where Christ is never found?

As followers of the crucified Christ, we are not filled by the world in which we live. A ship lives in the water, but if the water gets into the ship, the ship goes to the bottom. So you are to live in the world; but if the world takes possession of you, the ship of your life will sink.

Know, though, that self-denial is not the heart of Lent and Good Friday; Christ is. You will miss the purpose of our whole Lenten pilgrimage toward renewal if you encourage self-denial for its own sake. Note how St. Paul makes the transition from the section containing our text to the next section: "We were therefore buried with him through baptism into death in order that, just as Christ was raised from the dead through the glory of the Father, we too may live a new life" (Rom. 6:4). Self-denial is only a means to an end—the life of sanctification that the Holy Spirit works within us. The end is to be a "little Christ," to lead the "Christ-life." The Holy Spirit alone, working in you, makes that possible.

Devotion

Finally, the most distinguishing mark of your Christian life is *devotion*. It is the reason for your detachment, the background for your decision, the root of your self-denial—all empowered by the Holy Spirit.

As you have faithfully done during Lent, so in the days ahead learn time and again from your Savior how to devote time for periods of quietude, for mental and spiritual rest and refreshment. A medical doctor speaking to a church group once said, "Great poems, great masterpieces of literature, art, and sculpture, and great compositions of music are not given to the world by 'persons out of breath.'" Scripture emphasizes this when it says, "Be still, and know that I am God" (Ps. 46:10). "Those who wait on the LORD Shall renew *their* strength" (Is. 40:31 NKJV).

May you on this sacred Good Friday night appraise yourself and appreciate your Lord and his dearly won redemptive work for the forgiveness of your sins. May you sigh with the psalmist, "Search me, O God, and know my heart; test me and know my anxious thoughts. See if there is any offensive way in me, and lead me in the way everlasting" (Ps. 139:23–24).

Conclusion

Good Friday is a time for renewal of faith—a faith marked by detachment from the world, renewed decision for Christ, self-denial, and devotion in total faithfulness to him. Lift your eyes to the cross and ponder its meaning. Here is One dying willingly for the sins that you willingly committed against him—today, this past week, all the days of your life. By his dying, he forgives you. How can you ever fully know what that means? And yet, by the Holy Spirit's guidance and blessing, you can move ahead tonight and through all the days to come into an ever more deeply renewed faith in God's solemn promise and benediction, "[You] are justified freely by [God's] grace through the redemption that came by Christ Jesus. God presented him as a sacrifice of atonement, through faith in his blood" (Rom. 3:24).

Is Yours a Life of "Practical Atheism"?
Hebrews 4:14–5:10

[This sermon is offered as a second message for Good Friday. It also is adaptable for use in an Easter Eve service. In the latter case references to the Easter Vigil would of course be incorporated.]

A missionary once visited an isolated Appalachian mountain home. As he talked to the family living there, he discovered they had never heard the Gospel. When he had finished telling about Christ's suffering and death, the mother in the family leaned forward and said, "You say all this happened many years ago?"

"Yes," the minister answered. "Almost 2,000 years ago."

"And they nailed him to the cross when he had done nothing to hurt them and had even loved his enemies?"

"Yes," the minister replied.

And the lady said, "Well, let's hope it's not so." (Source unknown.)

Well, Christ's death on Good Friday *is* so. And in this hour you are confronted by the greatest event that has ever happened—for you. The great God-Man—forsaken by his friends, forsaken by the religious leaders of his day, forsaken by his countrymen, and finally forsaken by his heavenly Father—has earned your redemption! He has earned grace and mercy and forgiveness for you—just the help you need (v. 16).

But do you know what the tragedy of today is? Not merely that Christ's disciples and friends left him. Not merely that the church rejected him. Not merely that his country outlawed him. The real tragedy is that you and I, knowing all this, can still live every day as if it all never happened. We can lead lives of "practical atheism," rejecting Christ as the heart and center of our lives.

And the wonder is this: That in spite of our rejection, the great miracle of Good Friday confronts us: "God has shown us how much he loves us—it was while we were still sinners that Christ died for us" (Rom 5:8 TEV).

[Theme:] <u>We often live as though Good Friday never happened, but Christ *has* suffered and died—for us!</u> What a God! What a forgiveness! What a difference from the way we treat one another every day!

Blood Research

Our text speaks of our Lord Jesus Christ as our high priest. In Jesus' day, the high priest was the go-between, the middle-man between the people and God. Without him, there was no access to God. By God's command, he sacrificed animals, and their blood was shed in the atonement for sin. Blood: symbolic of life—and death.

A tragic instance when blood could have saved a person's life took place on April 1, 1950. Dr. Charles Richard Drew, a black physician and scientist, was killed in an auto accident on that day. His life might have been saved if the door had not been closed to him at the all-white hospital, which had a blood bank. But he was denied help and died—at the age of 46. The irony was that his research on banked blood had earlier contributed much to plasma research, which had saved countless lives. But Richard Drew was denied the benefits of his own discoveries because he was "different." (Source unknown.)

Our Lord also was engaged in "blood research." His life's blood has given new life to millions. Because of his "donation" people will live forever. But he was rejected because he was "different." He did not go along with the crowd. He not only spoke the "Good" but did it. He not only lived the letter of the law, but the spirit of it. He was different because where there was hate and evil, he was goodness incarnate—and so they killed him for it. And even as he suffered and died at the hands of men, he was different enough to forgive them for it.

Yes, our high priest was different. What a rejection! What a love!

The Real Tragedy

In the early days of the filming of the television series "This Is the Life," the players often discussed the script at great length with Rev. Herman W. Gockel, the religious advisor. One particular day, Randy Stuart, who played the young daughter in the Fisher family, asked Dr. Gockel, "Tell me, why do you always say Jesus 'died for us'? What do you mean, he 'died for us'? Why is that so important in the script?" (Personal comment by Herman W. Gockel to the author.)

That is the real tragedy of Good Friday, isn't it? So many people know the words but can't or don't apply them to their own sins. And it's not just others, but often you and I do this.

What have you done this week—something for which you've asked God to forgive you in the past—but which you went right ahead and did again anyway? Where might you have been different from others in an ethical decision in your work—but you went right ahead and did what others expected from you anyway? What plans did you make, what despair did you go through, what loneliness and fear did you suffer because you lived as if God didn't exist or actually care for you—all his promises to the contrary?

The real tragedy of Good Friday is not only that Christ was crucified years ago, but that you and I often crucify him again in our hearts. We reject our high priest as Lord of our lives, as One who now loves and forgives us and who wants to be Grace and Help for us—just when we need him (v. 16).

The Man Within

A classic example of a person who lived totally for self, as if God didn't really exist at all, is in Graham Greene's novel *The Man Within* (quoted by R. W. B. Lewis in *The Picaresque Saint* [New York: J. B. Lippencott Company, 1961]). In one fascinating scene Francis Andrews, a negativistic, indifferent character, turns on Elizabeth for not yielding to him before marriage. She replies:

> "You can't understand. It's not what you call respectability. It's a belief in God. I can't alter that for you. I'd leave you first."
> "What has he done for you?"
> Her candor was evident to him in the manner in which she met his challenge. She did not sweep it aside in a rush of words as some pious women might have done. She was silent, seeking an answer … and at last with a faint note of apology she brought out the brief reply, "I am alive."

What a profound, poignant statement! "I am alive!" Do you thank God for that sheer fact today—that you are physically as well as spiritually alive? We need to repent and remember who we are and whose we are and where every blessing of life has come from. "The life I live in the body, I live by faith in the Son of God, who loved me and gave himself for me" (Gal. 2:20).

Just When We Need It

There is good news in our text. "Our High Priest is not one who cannot feel sympathy for our weaknesses ... Let us be brave, then, and approach God's throne, where there is grace. There we will receive mercy and find grace to help us just when we need it" (4:15–16 TEV).

You and I can never fully comprehend the mystery and the depth of Christ's love that he enacts as our high priest and in our Savior, who became "the source of eternal salvation for all those who obey him" (5:9 TEV). But you and I do know by the power of the Holy Spirit that because he suffered for us, we will not suffer in separation from our heavenly Father through all eternity. Because he endured the loneliness of hell for us, we do know that we need not be forever lonely. We do know that we need not be forever fearful, for he faced the most fearful of foes—Satan and death itself—for us.

And that—the blessed result of Good Friday—has down-to-earth meaning for your life and my life every day. The reality of Christ's high priestly work for us is present and contemporary, not delayed and remote. Through his promise you and I are in eternity now.

A 6-year-old girl was suffering from terminal cancer. She had very little time left before she would die, and the time she did have was destined to be humiliating and painful. The effects of the cancer were visible to the eyes of all who looked at her. Tubes ran in and out of her tiny frame; the soft blonde hair that she once possessed was now gone, leaving her as a sight only to be pitied by those who dared to look. But, surprisingly, her sad circumstances did not take away her joy of life and the beautiful smile she wore each day.

One day, however, as a pastor was visiting her, he noticed that she was not in her usual cheerful state. Thinking that it was simply because of the intense pain of her physical body, the pastor dismissed the change until he saw tears forming. "What's the matter?" asked the pastor. With a maturity and confidence unmatched by many adults, she said, "I'm going to have a new body soon in heaven." "That's right," said the pastor, "but that's happy news. Why are you crying?" And with profound wisdom the tiny 6-year-old girl shocked the pastor when she uttered, "I'm going to have a new body when I get to heaven, but Jesus will always have the scars."

How is it that a small cancer-ridden child can recognize the Gospel and its essential truth, and we often remain unmoved and uncomforted in our pain? (Ray Cichocki, (†) in *Seasonal Illustrations,* 1991, 47)

That child-like insight is yours by the power of the Holy Spirit.

The Light of Victory

What are the Good Fridays of your life, those bleak days when you don't sense the blessings of Good Friday, fulfilled in Easter, in your heart?

In these days, cling to the hope God gives in our text. "Hold firmly to the faith we profess" (4:14 TEV). By the power of the Spirit, be brave, for "there is grace" (v. 16). God himself assures you, you will receive mercy "when [you] need it" (v. 16).

Throughout Scripture he promises help for your Good Fridays. "No temptation has seized you except what is common to man. And God is faithful; he will not let you be tempted beyond what you can bear. But when you are tempted, he will also provide a way out so that you can stand up under it" (1 Cor. 10:13). "As your days, so shall your strength be" (Deut. 33:25 RSV). "Underneath are the everlasting arms" (Deut. 33:27).

You need not feel guilty. Christ our high priest has taken your guilt upon himself. You need not be lonely. This suffering and victorious Christ says, "I am with you alway, even unto the end of the world" (Matt. 28:20 KJV). Nor need you fear. For "if God be for us, who can be against us?" (Rom. 8:31 KJV).

Good Friday and Easter have happened, indeed are happening right now, in your heart. As Christ your high priest leads you through the dark temple veil of Good Friday to Easter, may you live not in the gloom of defeat but in the radiant light of victory. Christ has died and risen for you. Your lifeblood has been restored. Daily reliving your Baptism, rejoicing in the Eucharist, and drinking from the "milk of the Word," you are different—from this day forward.

The Greatest News You Ever Heard

1 Corinthians 15:1-11

It was the darkest hour—just before dawn. Three women were making their way towards a tomb hewn in a rocky hillside outside the city. One of them spoke. "I still think it's a mistake to do this. Our enemies would love to catch us and destroy us all. Suppose they're hiding near the tomb and accuse us of trying to steal the body."

Another said, "Well, we'll just have to show them the spices we have and say all we wanted to do was anoint his body for burial."

But a third said, "But how will we get to it? Who will roll away that big stone covering the entrance to the tomb?"

It is another Easter morning, 2,000 years later. Your alarm goes off, and with an extra burst of willpower, knowing it is Easter, you get out of bed. Perhaps you get a quick look at the newspaper, with its usual accounts of death and life, of local stress and global strife. Perhaps you hear several Easter choirs on the radio on the way to church. And your mind wanders to your plans for this afternoon.

You and those three women 20 centuries ago have much in common. No one expects anything unusual to happen this morning. But the women were wrong. The stone already had been rolled away from the tomb, and an angel told them that Christ was risen from the dead.

You may have heard this message many times. But I say that the news is the most earthshaking, the most wonderful announcement you will ever hear. In a time of death and near-death, you and I have life—life now in this risen Christ and life with him which will never end.

The Easter message tells us many wonderful things. It tells us that Jesus is God, not just a martyred symbol of kindness who lived years ago; his resurrection was the crowning miracle of his ministry. Easter tells us also that Christ's promises are sure. He said he would rise in three days—and he did. And it tells us that humanity's salvation is assured. "Christ died for our sins in accordance with the scriptures" (v. 3 RSV). Christ's death on Calvary is complete. We are forgiven, at one with our Creator, and now we can again call him our Father.

But even more: Easter tells us that death is not the end. Because of Christ's death and resurrection an incredible promise is made to "you who believe." Yes [theme], <u>if you thought not much is going to happen here today, hear the promise God is making today: Though you one day will die, you will also live forever!</u> That is the Easter Gospel "which you [have] received, in which you stand, [and] by which you are saved"—when you "hold it fast," as our text here charges you (vv. 1–2 RSV).

Spiritual Death

A moment ago we noted that we live in a time of death and near-death. A TV program is interrupted, and we hear that a popular entertainer has been killed. "I can't believe he's dead," we say to each other. We go to work and learn a friend had a heart attack. "Why, I talked with him just hours ago," we recall.

Death may surprise us, but it is real. We may try to ignore it or delay it, but the fact remains (as a surgeon told some seminarians), "Do not forget … that with all the advances in medical science, the mortality rate remains at 100 percent."

But there is another kind of death which is also real and just as deadly, but subtly so. It is spiritual death—which we may not even know has occurred.

It is no news that millions of people live as if Good Friday and Easter never happened. Forty percent of the people in the United States identify with no church. J. Russell Hale interviewed a number of these people for his study *Who Are the Unchurched?* (Atlanta: Glenmary Research Center, 1977, reprinted by Concordia Theological Seminary Press, Fort Wayne, Indiana). He describes them as the Anti-Institutionalists, the Boxed-In, the Burned-Out, the Cop-Outs, the Happy Hedonists, the Locked-Out, the Nomads, the Pilgrims, the Publicans, the Scandalized, the True Unbelievers, and the Uncertain.

One intriguing discovery in his interviews was that many people considered themselves Christians but just didn't see the need for the church or for all that the Christian faith involves. But this diffidence, indifference, and lack of commitment to the way of our Lord Jesus Christ is goodness without godliness. How tragic, when millions around us fail to realize that what "goodness" they have is only a cultural legacy. It is really a habit formed by the accumulat-ed faith of Christian families and churches. They are feeding on the respectable life which the historic Christian church has built up, even though they ignore that church and belie/misrepresent its faith. Indeed, they are "drinking from a stream, the source of which they deny." Our Lord's dire promise applies to those who deny "the Lord that bought them, and bring upon themselves swift destruction" (2 Peter 2:1 KJV).

Then there are those, somewhat similar to the examples of "goodness without godliness," who have some contact with the church, but for whom it is a "religion without repentance." They show a flurry of interest periodically—when the church is called in for a Baptism or a wedding or a funeral. As one "Happy Hedonist" said when he phoned a Christian neighbor on Christmas Eve, "When does your Christmas Eve service start? I thought I'd surprise you all and just drop in tonight and 'pay my dues' and put a little something in your collection."

But with Christmas or Easter over, with the baby baptized, the son or daughter married, the grandparent buried—with these flashes of the appearance of piety over, it's back to business as usual. A dash of religion—but without repentance.

Spiritual death—that's what we're talking about. It's not only "out there"; *the greatest peril of the church is always from with-in.* Too often, almost all of us in the church accept the Easter Gospel noetically, up in our heads, but do little about a resurrected life lived out for others in the world. Most of us say we believe Christ rose from the dead, but do we "believe in vain" (v. 2) because we're not really "holding fast" (v. 2 RSV) to that truth by a changed life which makes Easter a daily reality?

Robert Herhold once wrote in *Learning to Die/Learning to Live:*

> I just watched a rerun of "All in the Family." Four adults shouted at each other constantly for 27 minutes. My uneasiness betrays the fact that I can be as unreasonable as Archie and as quarrelsome as Mike. I protest physical violence, yet I practice psychological vio-lence. When will I ever realize that life is as short as … as a televi-sion program? Only there are no reruns. (Philadelphia: Fortress Press, 1976, 66)

Are we living resurrected lives? Are we laying down our lives in sacrificial living, as our Savior did for us? Are we following his way when the tests and temptations of life beset us? Or are we letting the world "squeeze us into its own mould" rather than letting God "re-mould us from within" as his new creation in a resurrected life (see Rom. 12:2, JBP)?

Yes, spiritual death is real.

Hope—"In Which You Stand"

But right at this point lies our Easter hope. It is in realizing our desperate condition that we discover the *Good* News, not the bad. You who have made the Lenten pilgrimage in your heart again this year have seen your Savior suffering and dying on Calvary's lonely hill. And you have known that it was for your sins that he died and that it was your death that he died (cf. v. 3).

An atheist who served as a custodian at a seminary enjoyed baiting the young theologians. He told one who was reading a book about eternal life, "If you ask me, that's so much hogwash. When you're dead, you're dead." The student replied, "You're right, George. When you're dead, you're dead." The janitor walked away, wondering what in the world that young man was doing at a seminary. The student's point was that hope of eternal life comes only *after* one has faced the reality of *eternal* death—which the janitor had not.

In a sense, "It's too bad that dying is the last thing we do, because it could teach us so much about living," said Robert Herhold. However, in Christ, we have faced spiritual death—and the death of dying to ourselves is not the last thing we do. By repentance by the power of the Holy Spirit, we have learned much about living. We have experienced the blessed reality of the Easter miracle "by which [we] are saved" (v. 2 RSV). And we do not believe in vain (v. 2), for Christ is the Lord of death and gives us a new life in and through himself—today! You and I cannot ultimately be destroyed by either physical death or a spiritual death!

Our text for today from 1 Corinthians does not detail the life to come which Christ's resurrection seals for us, but the rest of Scripture beautifully affirms the truth of our eternal life with our Lord—a life that will be free of all fear. Just think of it! You will live again! You've heard people say, "You only live once." How different the comment of a faithful old saint nearing death and telling her pastor, "Pastor, isn't it wonderful that this isn't the only life we have?"

Your life is eternal—literally, it will never end. It will be free of all that death entails: disease, decay, disintegration. Second, it will be a life free of all fear. For Christ himself entered the darkness of death and broke its chains. He is like the wise father who knows his child's fear of the darkness. He does not tease the child, but goes into a dark room for a while, then comes out saying, "See, there is really nothing to be afraid of. Now come, take my hand, and we'll go in together."

And there is no fear because, third, it is life with the Lord. It's like a young girl's retelling of the story of Enoch. She said, "Well, God and Enoch were good friends, and they used to take long walks together. And one day God said, 'Enoch, you are tired. Come into my house and stay and rest a while.'" What comfort for those who have lost loved ones to know that they are now just "staying and resting a while" with the Lord! (Source unknown.)

Until then we live here to Christ. Our Easter faith changes our whole perspective on this side of the grave. Since we know we are going to die physically, we can live with a certain zest and vividness—and a fascination that comes from knowing we have the things of this life only for a while. So we sense both satisfaction and detachment about the experience. Indeed, as pilgrims, you and I have a certain tang in our life and work that unbelievers cannot have.

Therefore, I challenge you this Easter morning to live as one who must die, knowing God will take care of you—and to work each day, knowing you have the privilege of bringing to others this joyous Easter news of a resurrected Savior, who frees us from fear of death and empowers us to live new, resurrected lives.

There once was a family that lost three of its four children within just two weeks to a virulent disease. One child was left, a 4-year-old boy. The family had buried the third child just two weeks before Easter. On Easter morning the parents and remaining child went to church. The mother told her Sunday school class about the resurrection of Christ. The father read the Easter story in Sunday school as he led the devotions. People who knew of their great loss wondered how they could do it.

On the way home, a 16-year-old youth asked his father, "Dad, that couple must really believe everything about the Easter story, don't they?"

"Of course they believe it," said the father. "All Christians do."

"But not as *they* do," said the youth. (Source unknown.)

And you: Do you "really believe it"—as they did? But more: Do you live it? And by the power of the resurrected Christ, are you ready to go out and make life around you a little Easter wherever you work and live by witnessing to him by your words and deeds?

This is your Easter challenge. Maybe like those women on that first Easter day, you didn't expect too much to happen here today. But God has called out to you through his Holy Word. And where God is at work, anything can happen!

God breaks through to you with the certainty that physical death need not frighten you. Your life may be difficult, but its burdens cannot crush you. Instead, life can be joyful, for Christ lives!

For because Christ died, you need not fear to die.

Because Christ rose, you can live a resurrected life every day.

And because he lives forever, you will live—and reign—with him into all eternity!

Are You Living the "Ascended" Life?

Hebrews 5:7-9

A group of Japanese high school students were on a tour of the United States. As they went through busy air terminals, bus and railway stations, their leader told them, "I will hold a Japanese flag high above my head as we work our way through the crowds. Just keep an eye on that flag, and *you won't get lost*!"

When the group returned to Japan, a teacher asked them, "What is the one thing you remember most about your trip to the United States of America?"

"The Japanese flag!" they chorused in unison. (*Seasonal Illustrations,* 155-56)

Christ is our flag, and on this day we look to him as he ascends into heaven. But we also ask, "Now what?" Hans Küng answered that we are not just to "look up to heaven in amazement but bear witness to Jesus in the world." (*On Being a Christian* [New York: Doubleday, 1984], 352, 354) We are not just to stand around and bemoan the departure of our Lord; but like the early disciples, we are to evidence his living presence and embody his Great Commission in action. They were ready to fulfill Christ's last words, "Ye shall be witnesses unto me" (Acts 1:8 KJV).

So I ask you, if you are to be a witness to the Lord of life, what do people see when they look at you? Do they see the marks of a Christian?

My theme: <u>Although we are often proud, lifeless in our devotion, disobedient to God, and do not lead ascended lives, God calls us to humility, devotion, and obedience to him.</u>

The Marks of a Christian

Humility, devotion, and obedience: The marks of a Christian come from Christ himself. As our text spells out, "In his life on earth Jesus made his prayers and requests with loud cries and tears to God, who could save him from death. Because he was humble and devoted, God heard him. But even though he was God's Son, he learned through his sufferings to be obedient. When

71

he was made perfect, he became the source of eternal salvation for all those who obey him" (Heb. 5:7–9 TEV).

Note those last words: He is "the source of eternal salvation for all those who obey him" (v. 9 TEV). Paul puts it beautifully in his letter to the Galatian Christians (2:19b–20 TEV), "I have been put to death with Christ on his cross, so that it is no longer I who live, but it is Christ who lives in me. This life that I live now, I live by faith in the son of God, who loved me and gave his life for me."

Note well: We are saved totally through our faith in Jesus Christ, not by any of our own doing. Now, that being granted, what are some of the characteristics of our Lord's life which he calls us to follow?

We are not just speaking of virtues to emulate. That is the evil of moralism. Moralism exalts a value as a way one achieves spirituality. Biblical Christianity sees any virtues as results of the Gospel active in the believer's life.

Further, Christ is not just guide, model, or example. He is prototype. We focus not on his humility as a precept to follow, but on his humiliation, his sacrifice for us. Morally, we fail totally. But through his death and resurrection we are forgiven and then called to the fruits of faith, empowered solely by the Holy Spirit (see Galations 5 and 6). Christ as prototype is the first fruits of those who believe in him. The Christian life, then, is "Christ in me," a concept Paul uses some 32 times in the New Testament (see, e.g., Col. 1:27).

What then are the marks of our Lord here?

Humility

Our text says, "In his life on earth Jesus made his prayers and requests with loud cries and tears to God, who could save him from death. Because he was humble and devoted, God heard him" (v. 7 TEV). Note those first two blessed qualities in our Lord's life: humility and devotion.

Humility. As the writer to the Hebrews puts it, "Think of what he went through; how he put up with so much hatred from sinners! So do not let yourselves become discouraged and give up" (Heb. 12:3 TEV).

Humility. Is it a distinguishing mark of your life? Remember the classic comment, "Oh, he's very humble; he's got so much to be humble about!"

Humility. It means a quiet recognition of the capacities which God has given you—balanced by your limitations. It means knowing your shortcomings but making a full and responsible use of your abilities—to the glory of God. Scripture says in effect, "Accept the limits of personality potential with which God has endowed you. God is not interested in success as it is measured by competition. God is concerned that a person's life be developed to the fullness of its potential."

Do you want to overcome your anxiety which flows from a sense of inadequacy in this age of competitive supremacy? Then make this insight your own: *Stop competing with others.* Rather, remember that it is required in stewards that a person be found *faithful*—not always effective or successful, but faithful. In faithful humility, dedicate yourself to the service of God, in whatever position of life you may be.

Devotion

Humility—and *devotion.* Can you honestly say that your life is one characterized by devotion? Have you learned from our Savior how to take time for periods of quietude, for mental and spiritual rest? Examine your frame of mind right now. Are you totally open to what God wants to say to you, or are other things on your mind?

Imagine a student coming to worship this morning, carrying a high stack of books and the work he has to do. Include in the scene a businesswoman arriving with a computer, and someone staring out an open church window at a car engine that needs attention. Imagine that everyone brought work to church. This afternoon, one of these people likely would say to another, "You know, I didn't get a thing out of the service this morning, did you?" And the other would answer, "No, I didn't either." Once you realize how easy it is to do this mentally on Sunday morning, you realize how much more easily it happens during the week when you want to set aside some time for Bible study, prayer, and the reading of Christian literature.

The real problem is that many of us don't see a need for or a value from daily use of God's Word. God, however, wants to bless us every day. The means he uses is his Word—straight in Scripture and/or explained in devotionals and other religious books. Spend time with him daily, and you will know and experience the blessings—the strength, joy, and peace—he has for you.

Obedience

Humility, devotion—and *obedience*. "But even though he was God's Son, he learned through his sufferings to be obedient" (Heb. 5:8 TEV). As Christ was obedient to his heavenly Father, are you obedient to him?

A pastor tells the story of a sprightly old lady who suddenly developed breast cancer and was facing surgery on her 65th birthday. Her husband had been dead for many years. Her mother, a venerable saint, had died in the Lord at 87, having spent the last 18 years of her life in a wheelchair, her right side totally paralyzed. How often, the pastor said, they had both recalled her rugged, indomitable faith!

And now the daughter, with the years coming on, faced surgery the next morning. They sat in the sun-room of the hospital. She said, "I'm not really afraid at all, Pastor. I've had a rich and full life. God has been so good to me. This breast cancer is quite a surprise to me, but it hasn't gotten me down. I have the finest of doctors. And whichever way it turns out, that's fine with me. Either way—I accept it."

She said the words calmly, yes, confidently, said the pastor. What a radiant, relaxed faith she had! She was not saying her illness—or possible death—were the will of God. Illness and death come because we are sinful, mortal persons. But she was saying, "I rest in you, O Lord!" What an example of humble, devoted Christian obedience! (*You Say You're Depressed?* 106–7)

How do you and I learn such obedience? By suffering! Be sure to read through the first letter from Peter. There's a lot of down-to-earth perspective there in putting suffering into a proper perspective. There's the whole section in 1 Peter 2: "God will bless you for this, if you endure the pain of undeserved suffering because you are conscious of his will. ... If you endure suffering even when you have done right, God will bless you for it. It was to this that God called you, for Christ himself suffered for you and left you an example, that you would follow in his steps" (1 Peter 2:19–21 TEV). And in 1 Peter 4:1: "Since Christ suffered physically, you too must strengthen yourselves with the same way of thinking" (TEV). And verses 12–13: "My dear friends, do not be surprised at the painful test you are suffering, as though something unusual were happening to you. Rather be glad that you are sharing Christ's sufferings, so that you may be full of joy when his glory is revealed" (TEV).

Joy? Joy in suffering? I can just guess what you're thinking, "That's just too glib to put into practice!" Yet Job said, "Though he slay me, yet will I trust in him" (Job 13:15 KJV). A woman whose mother, oldest, and youngest sisters had all died of cancer (and who suspected the potentiality in herself!) said, "Pain is pain, but it does draw you closer to God."

A woman doctor in Oakland, California, told her pastor, "I thank God for giving me tuberculosis. I had wandered far away from him for years. But lying on this hospital bed all these months has brought me up sharply again to remember *who* I am and *whose* I am and *where* I am going. Thank God I got TB!" (Personal conversation with the author.)

Christ the Source of Salvation

So the inspired writer concludes, "When he was made perfect, he became the source of eternal salvation for all those who obey him" (Heb. 5:9 TEV). Christ is perfect. He is the source of our life and salvation.

Elsewhere in this letter the divine writer puts it poignantly, "As for us, we have this large crowd of witnesses around us. So then, let us rid ourselves of everything that gets in the way, and of the sin which holds on to us so tightly, and let us run with determination the race that lies before us. Let us keep our eyes fixed on Jesus, on whom our faith depends from beginning to end. He did not give up because of the cross! On the contrary, because of the joy that was waiting for him, he thought nothing of the disgrace of dying on the cross, and he is now seated at the right side of God's throne" (Heb. 12:1–2 TEV). By the power of the Holy Spirit may that be fulfilled: "Christ in you."

Look to Jesus, "the author and finisher of our faith" (Heb. 12:2 KJV). Jesus Christ is no mere symbol of love, no mere example to follow. Listen: "Christ himself carried our sins in his body to the cross, so that we might die to sin and live for righteousness. It is by his wounds that you have been healed" (1 Peter 2:24 TEV).

Christ died for your sins and mine. He is the source of our life and salvation. By his power in us, we are "those who obey him" (Heb. 5:9 TEV). We realize that "the man whose life is lived in love does, in fact, live in God, and God does, in fact, live in him. So our love for him grows more and more, filling us with complete confidence for the day when he shall judge all men—for we realise that our life in this world is actually his life lived in us" (1 John 4:16–17 JBP).

And there's the summation—and the source—of these three marks of a Christian as we gaze at our Lord on this Ascension Day: humility, devotion, and obedience. They all flow out of the love of God on Calvary, implanted in our hearts. No moralism here! Christ is no mere example, for we are unable to follow. We can do nothing. It is he who forgives us, who lives in us, and who comes to us daily in his Word, in our Holy Baptism, in the Blessed Eucharist, and in Holy Absolution. And now we, as Luther said, are to be "little Christs." "By this all will know that you are My disciples, if you have love for one another" (John 13:35 NKJV).

Living It Out

So—as you continue on in your life, how can you—by the Holy Spirit's power—live out these marks of Christ's character? How can you be a true carbon copy of him when so many problems and questions and doubts assail you? Imagine you are walking on a suburban street and see three little children, all under the age of five, in the back of a station wagon. The luggage rack on top of the car is loaded with baggage. The father is just closing the garage door, the mother shutting the front door. It is obvious the family is leaving on a trip.

You walk up to the little children and say, "Where are you going?" Wide-eyed they stare back at you. They don't know.

"What highway are you taking?" No answer.

"Where are you going to have dinner tonight?" No response.

"Where are you going to sleep tonight?" Still no reply.

"With whom are you going?" you ask.

Their eyes light up, their faces break into smiles.

"With Mommy and Daddy!" they exclaim.

Those children didn't have the answers to your questions. But they knew with whom they were going. And that was enough for them. (*The Best of Your Life,* 35)

And you: Your life lies ahead of you. There are many unknowns. For many of the questions you have, you have no answers. But you do have the Answerer, the ascended Christ, with you. He is by your side, every step of the way. Do you really need anything more?

"Wake Up, Dry Bones!"
Ezekiel 37:1-3, 11-14

The college student sat in her dorm room, staring out the window. The campus pastor [the author] sat nearby. The girl's voice was choked with pain and misery. "Why doesn't God speak to me? I feel so hollow, so empty, so alone. Where is God? Why doesn't he come to me? I feel so lifeless—like a bag of bones."

The pastor looked at the dorm room walls. Books and more books. No picture of Christ on the wall. No Bible in sight. Draped over a chair was a sweatshirt with the words "I am a virgin." Underneath in small letters were the words "However, this is a very old shirt."

Quietly the pastor began to speak. "When was the last time you read your Bible with an open mind and a penitent heart? When was the last time you recalled your Baptism and relived God's promise to you of new life each day through his Holy Spirit?"

The young woman sighed and ran her hand through her curly blonde hair. The pastor continued. "God is not a 'god of the zaps.' He doesn't just 'zap' you with answers out of the blue. He comes through the channels of his Holy Spirit. He comes through the means of his grace, his Word and sacraments. When was the last time you went to Holy Communion—with joy? When was the last time you went to private confession to receive the individualized absolution of God's grace?"

The woman stared out of the window.

Have you ever felt like that young woman—lifeless, empty, alone? Our text tells us a story about dry bones. But it also tells us how our lives of hollowness and emptiness can be made alive again and how dry bones can be made into living flesh—by God the Holy Spirit, who revives and restores us daily and resurrects us for the life to come.

Today is Pentecost, signifying 50 days after Easter. It is also called Whitsunday, or White-Sunday, since in former centuries the new members of the church who were baptized or confirmed on this day had the custom of wearing white robes.

One of the three chief festivals of the Christian Church, today, Pentecost, is just as important as Christmas and Easter, for today we focus on the work of the Holy Spirit. He it was who first called you to faith, brought you into God's family in Holy Baptism, and continually comes to you in the means of grace. But because of our sinful nature, you and I are inclined to fall away from faith. And so our theme: <u>Though we often feel lifeless, God the Holy Spirit revives us and restores us daily and resurrects us for the life to come.</u>

Dry Bones

This word from the prophet Ezekiel is actually a prophecy of how God will resurrect the children of Israel from their grave of bondage to the Babylonian people. Note how the dramatic scene builds up. God takes Ezekiel to the middle of a valley covered with bones. They are dry, for they have been there a long time. In this scene of absolute and utter hopelessness and despair God gives a word of hope to a hopeless people: He promises that they will arise. But this resurrection will only occur by the word of the Lord (Ezek. 37:4), for with God nothing is impossible. God speaks and so performs (v. 14).

Thanks be to God, he does the same in your life and my life today. You and I are like the children of Israel—lifeless, too often alone. But the Holy Spirit puts breath into our breathless bones by pointing us to the cross of him who died for us and rose again and who through Word and Sacrament comes to us again today.

A man lies on a hospital bed. "I feel so useless," he says. "I feel cut off from reality here. My life is like dust in my hands." Do you feel like that man?

A woman says, "My children are grown. My husband has his work. I spend many hours alone. What's the purpose of my life now?" Are you that woman?

A teenager bemoans, "I don't know who I am," he says. "What shall I do with my life? Where am I going? What's to become of me? Do my friends really like me—or do they just say they do?" Do you feel like that young man?

A young mother sighs, "I have no time for myself. Life is nothing but drudgery from one day to the next. I'm not growing inwardly. I had such different hopes and dreams for the future. My life is busy but really empty of meaning. Where am I going in my life?" Are you like that young mother?

A young worker complains, "How can I, with my supervisor constantly looking over my shoulder, stack boxes eight hours a day—to the glory of God?" Are you like that young worker?

Are you a bag of bones—dry bones, lifeless bones, dead bones? Are you cut off from life as it was meant to be, with no hope? Scripture tells us we need to repent

- for failing to see God as source of our life. *"It is* He *who* has made us, and not we ourselves" (Ps. 100:3 NKJV).
- for failing to trust in him, not ourselves. "It is God who works in you both to will and to do for *His* good pleasure" (Phil. 2:13 NKJV).
- for failing to use his means of grace as the power supply for our daily lives. "You do not have what you want because you do not ask God for it" (James 4:2 TEV).
- for failing to see him as the one who will also raise these dry bones on the last day (Ezek. 37:12).

This is our greatest problem: We often don't repent or faithfully use the means of grace.

Living Flesh

But God promises, "Your strength will equal your days" (Deut. 33:25). "Underneath are the everlasting arms" (v. 27). "Do not be dismayed, for I am your God. I will strengthen you and help you; I will uphold you with my righteous right hand" (Is. 41:10). "Come, all you who are thirsty, come to the waters; and you who have no money, come, buy and eat! Come, buy wine and milk without money and without cost" (Is. 55:1).

God is a discoverable, contemporary God. He lovingly desires us to use the power supply of his Word and Sacraments, to be open to his Holy Spirit who would turn our dry bones into living flesh (Ezek. 37:6).

How does this take place?

1. Through use of his Word.

A little girl picked up a dust-covered Bible. "Mommy, whose book is this?" she asked.

"Oh, it's God's book," said the mother piously.

"Well," the girl replied, "we'd better send it back to him

because we're not using it."

Why not keep your Bibles open in your homes that you might be more inclined to "take up and read"? There you will find the fresh milk of the Word that you may grow thereby. For this Word of God is "the power of God for the salvation of everyone who believes" (Rom. 1:16). It will put flesh on your bones and joy into an otherwise sagging spirit.

2. Relive your Baptism each day.

In Holy Baptism you were first made a member of the family of God and of his body, the church. Your daily memory of it will lead you to Calvary and then to the empty tomb so that you can be raised with Christ to a newness of life. "All of us who were baptized into Christ Jesus were baptized into his death ... that, just as Christ was raised from the dead through the glory of the Father, we too may live a new life" (Rom. 6:3-4). Yes, through our Baptism we have the forgiveness of sins.

3. Go to the Lord's Supper with joy every time it's offered.

We don't go just when we feel "worthy" of going. The Sacrament of Holy Communion is for sinners like you and me. And as Luther said, "Your hunger and thirst [for it] will come as you receive, and the more you receive, the more you will hunger and thirst [for it]." Oh, may you discover again and again the blessings of regular communion and a deepening, active fellowship with him in his real presence in this Sacrament. There may you yield your whole being to that transcendent vision of the crucified Redeemer and thus enter into communion with Christ himself as you receive the forgiveness of your sins. For Christ will take you, penetrate you, and assimilate you to himself (Olin Alfred Curtis). In the semicircle of communicants in the chancel, you will be swept into mystical union with all the saints in heaven who complete that circle on the other side of the empty tomb.

4. Receive the personalized forgiveness in Private Confession and Holy Absolution.

There's another blessing available to you that is not often practiced in our churches, sad to say. That is the opportunity for private confession to a pastor. You need not confess specific sins in that situation, but you can make a general confession. And you will receive the benefit of an individualized absolution: "Your sins are forgiven you. Go in peace and joy!" As Luther said, "I will allow no man to take private confession away from me, and I would not give it up for all the treasures in the world, since I know what comfort and strength it has given me." ("On Private Confession" 1522, *Luther's Works* 51:98)

Why Do We Despair?

Years ago a ship on the Atlantic was in distress because its supply of fresh water had run out. The crew anticipated a horrible death from thirst, and that with water all around them. When hope was almost gone, they sighted a ship approaching them. At once they hoisted distress signals. But the only answer they got was "Dip it up."

"Dip it up?" What heartless mockery! To dip up buckets of salt water!

They signaled again but got the same answer. Finally in despair, they lowered a bucket. Imagine their amazement and joy when the water turned out to be fresh, living water. The sailors didn't know it, but they were at the mouth of the mighty Amazon River, whose fresh water flows far out to sea.

God's fresh living water in his means of grace—his Word and sacraments—is always there. Why do we despair? Dip it up! (*Seasonal Illustrations,* 114)

God Acts

Through his Word and the sacraments, God wants to breathe new life into you. "I will put my Spirit in you and you will live, and I will settle you in your own land. Then you will know that I the LORD have spoken, and I have done it, declares the LORD" (Ezek. 37:14).

Yes, the means of grace are there. God not only speaks, but acts. The promises of God are kept. And that's not only for today. The Spirit also assures us of the life to come. "Therefore prophesy and say to them: 'This is what the Sovereign LORD says: O my people, I am going to open your graves and bring you up from them. ... Then you will know that I the LORD have spoken, and I have done it" (Ezek. 37:12, 14).

Just after an early-morning Easter service, as a couple came out of the church, their little boy swung on the pastor's arm as he greeted them. A little while later the pastor received a phone call from the couple. Their boy had climbed the ladder into his bunk bed for a nap, fallen, hit his temple, and died instantly.

The pastor rushed to their home. The father met him at the front door and placed his dead son into the pastor's arms. "Where's the resurrection now?" he said, agony in his voice.

The pastor later concluded, "The only thing that held that couple together *was* the resurrection." They survived their tragedy and believed that they would see their son again. (Incident recounted to the author by a Midwestern pastor.)

Ezekiel gives you and me the same hope. "I will put my Spirit in you and you will live. ... Then you will know that I the LORD have spoken, and I have done it." You *do* have hope—for your life today and for the life to come.

Do you ever feel like a bag of bones? Do you want hope and life and a joyful spirit? Come, for all things are now ready.

"Here We Stand" or "Here We Go"?
Acts 1:8

[This sermon emphasizes personal reformation—especially in witnessing. Some of the material is from my sermon "Lent: A Time for Renewal of Witness," in *Lent: A Time for Renewal*, 93–96.]

A pastor, wearing his clerical collar, got on a plane in Seattle and settled down next to a man for about a three-hour trip to L. A. "Oh, my," the man said to himself. "A man of religion! I'll head him off." So he said aloud to the pastor, "I have a very simple philosophy about religion: 'Do unto others.'" And he thought he had silenced the clergyman. But the pastor was very gracious and said to the man, "I see you have a little button on your lapel. What is that?"

"Oh, I'm an astronomer," he replied. "I've just come back from a convention." The man continued talking about the latest research about outer space for almost the whole trip.

At the end of that time the pastor said, "Well that's all very interesting. But you know, I have a very simple philosophy about astronomy: 'Twinkle, Twinkle Little Star.'" (Story heard by the author.)

Well, astronomy isn't simple, and neither is religion. Nor is being a Christian in today's pagan world.

Here we are again at the time of celebration of the Reformation. How do we celebrate it? Why do we celebrate it?

One thing is clear. We didn't come here to worship Martin Luther. God could have used any humble man to start the Protestant Reformation.

The Blessings of the Reformation

No, we come here to thank and praise God for the blessings we have received in and through Martin Luther. And we could spend the next several minutes going into great detail on the nature of these blessings and how we are to make use of them in our lives today. Call them to mind once again:

1. The open Bible
2. Justification by grace through faith
3. The doctrine of the priesthood of all believers
4. The biblical doctrine of the Lord's Supper
5. Popular education, and Luther's writing of the catechisms
6. Our heritage of hymns and liturgy
7. Civil and religious liberty—Luther's stress on individual freedom and the right of private judgment

I'm sure you've heard sermons on these great blessings of the Reformation many times. But the question is: What are you and I doing with them?

Are you one of those in the church trying to set the clock back: "We'll stay by the old ways"?

Do you want to stop the clock: "I'll stay with the status quo; don't rock the boat"?

Or, are you one of those who wants to get with the clock, to move with time, to progress as a church in fulfilling Christ's Great Commission to reach people in a secular society with a relevant Gospel for the salvation of a lost humanity?

That's my theme: <u>Although we often fail to live out the blessings of the Reformation, God calls us to be his witnesses by going back to an open Bible and by being prepared to be a suffering church.</u>

The Open Bible

Do you, first of all, appreciate the blessing that came from the Reformation of an open Bible? Do you search Scripture daily? Is it alive for you, and do you share that living Word with others?

A man sitting in an airline terminal pulled a small New Testament from his pocket and started to read it. A man sitting near him saw him reading and said, "I don't go much for religion."

The first man replied, "Well, I feel you certainly are missing something."

"I don't see any sense," the other man continued, "in following a Christ that has been dead 2,000 years."

"What did you say?" answered the first man. "Christ—dead? Why, that couldn't be, for I was just talking to him a few minutes ago." (Source unknown.)

You, worshiping with us here today: Is Christ alive to you? The secret of coping with anxiety, fear, or any kind of emotional conflict, any defeat or difficulty, any hardship or sorrow, is to have the experience that man did. He found Christ was so alive in his Word that he could talk with him any place, any time. Is Christ alive to you—as he was to that man hearing Christ speaking to him in his New Testament?

To paraphrase a prayer by Christina Georgina Rossetti (1830–1894), "Oh, Lord, reform your church, beginning with me. And by your Holy Spirit let me begin by once more being a student of the open Bible, which Luther opened up to all people in their language."

A Zipper on Your Lip?

Know your Bible better—and thus better know what to say to the people to whom God calls you to be a witness.

Several students were walking across the quadrangle of a large university just as the bell tower chimed 5:00 o'clock in the afternoon. At that precise moment a foreign student on the sidewalk in front of them dropped full length on the ground to the utter amazement of those walking behind him. After the initial shock the students realized that he had not stumbled or fallen but was a Muslim prostrating himself at his holy hour of prayer.

That man was not ashamed of his religion. How many of you are not ashamed to make known that you are a Christian? How many of us, by omitting prayer or other practices that might let others know we are Christians, in effect become guilty of sinning, as Peter did when he said of Christ, "I don't know the man!" What a tragedy for those who have been nominal members of the church but about whom Christ will one day say, "I never knew you"!

Deny Christ in your life with explicit rejection of him as Peter did, and Christ will say on the Last Day, "I never knew you!" Or, deny Christ by keeping a zipper on your lip, like the people at the end of the gospel of Mark ("They said nothing to anyone, because they were afraid" [Mk. 16:8]). On the Last Day Christ will say, "I have nothing to say for you, either!" (*Bold Ones on Campus,* 63)

Two college students were talking about their summer jobs. One mentioned he would be working in a logging camp. "Well, you're going to have quite a time of it," said his companion. "All those rough men, cursing, drinking, and their ways with women. And you—a Christian."

The summer passed, each student completed his job, and they met on campus again. "Well," said the one student to the other. "How did you get along in that rough mining camp with all those men? And you—a Christian?"

"Oh," replied the other student, "they never caught on!" (Source unknown.)

Will that be said at the end of your life—"They never caught on"?

A milk-truck driver came to a campus pastor and told him of a student attending his chapel who lived with the driver in his boarding house. Because of the example of that student's faith the man wanted to join the church. "That young man has a faith to live by," he said. "I want that faith." (*Bold Ones on Campus,* 167)

Could people say that about you?

When we examine ourselves, we must admit that we are often like Peter. We live as if to say, "I don't know the man." We need to repent.

Oh, Lord, reform your church, beginning with me.

Now—you and I may nod in agreement and admit that we have failed to be witnesses—"Yeah, I should share my faith more"—but too often we go home and do nothing.

The Logjam

Where's the logjam here? For one thing, as we've said, it's a matter of getting back into the Bible so that we know better what to say about our faith. But it's also a matter of overcoming our lack of preparedness and our fear of witnessing.

I'm not saying that each of you needs to go up and down the streets and ring the doorbells of strangers' homes like the Mormons and Jehovah's Witnesses (though there is a time for the right kind of evangelization canvassing). But you can, every day, live out far more convincingly who and what you are: a baptized, redeemed child of God—and tell other people who your real Father is. And you can let your Christian walk show far more in the natural relationships of your daily life.

Be what you are! A woman came up to a pastor after an evangelization presentation and said, "There's one thing in your talk that you said that really struck me. You said each of us is to witness if only in our own 'fumbling, stumbling' way. 'Fumbling, stumbling'—that's me!" (Comment made to author)

Oh, Lord, reform your church, beginning with me.

Natural Settings

In the natural setting of your workplace or your kitchen, or engaged in sports activities with your neighbors, or around the barbecue fires late at night, when your friends or neighbors ask their questions of "why" about life, tell them about Jesus and the resurrection. That's when to say,

> "I believe that Jesus Christ, true God, begotten of the Father from eternity, and also true man, born of the Virgin Mary, is my Lord, who has redeemed me, a lost and condemned person, purchased and won me from all sins, from death, and from the power of the devil; not with gold or silver, but with his holy, precious blood and with his innocent suffering and death, that I may be his own and live under him in his kingdom and serve him in everlasting righteousness, innocence, and blessedness, just as he is risen from the dead, lives and reigns to all eternity." (Luther's explanation of the Second Article)

Dr. Howard Kelly, famed surgeon and renowned for living as a Christian in his profession, always had a beautiful rosebud in the lapel of his coat. It remained fresh for a long time. When people asked him the secret, he turned the lapel and showed them a little glass vial containing water. The stem of the rose went through the button hole into the water and thus remained fresh for a longer time. And then Dr. Kelly would tell people that the secret of beautiful and fragrant Christian living was in drawing refreshment from the only true water of life, Jesus Christ, the one who forgives sins, the one who died for our sins and rose again. (Adapted from Wilbur E. Nelson, *Anecdotes and Illustrations,* [Grand Rapids: Baker Books, 1971], 44)

That water of life is yours now—and always has been—in your Baptism (Rom. 6:3-4). But now you are to tell others about that living water, to repeat God's invitation to everyone, "Come, all you who are thirsty, come to the waters; and you who have no money, come, buy and eat! Come, buy wine and milk without money and without cost" (Is. 55:1).

I agree, witnessing is not always easy. But Bible study with your fellow Christians will prepare you.

And you may face rejection by others. But Christ himself bore rejection for us. And he promised to be with us when we witness. Listen to God's powerful promise in Matthew 10:19, "Do not worry about what you are going to say or how you will say it; when the time comes, you will be given what you will say" (TEV). What a wonderful promise of God!

A Suffering Church

And finally, if you are going to be a re-formed Christian and take seriously the task of witnessing, you may have to suffer. I am not calling you to a life of masochism, self-pity, or martyrdom; but your witness may involve sacrifice.

Do you remember Christian Zimmermann, the pastor who was also the flight engineer on TWA flight 847, which was hijacked in the 1980s? He went through a lot of suffering in that hijacking, but he also dared to share his Christian faith with his hijackers. And his suffering is not over yet. He once told a friend, "Yesterday when I got up in the morning, the very first thought I had was of the young Navy man whom they murdered—and then threw his body out of the plane onto the ground."

Christian said he would ask his hijackers, "What do you believe?" After they told him, he would ask, "Now, what do you think I believe as a Christian?" And they would tell him, but then he would correct their misunderstanding about the Christian faith—and share the Gospel with them. (From a personal conversation with the author.)

You can do the same with your friends. Ask them what they believe, and listen; but then ask what they think you believe. Then you can tell them about the Christ who died to save them.

Even you high school students have opportunities for witnessing. Because the Equal Access Act of 1984 was passed by the U.S. Congress, you can now hold religious meetings on public high school campuses and have Bible studies and share your faith. Such groups cannot be church-sponsored or led by pastors, but you can, as our text says, "be [Christ's] witnesses" right on your own school campus every day.

Oh, Lord, reform your church, beginning with me.

In conclusion, go back with me to that first Christmas night, so many years ago, after the shepherds had seen the angels in the heavens announcing the birth of the Christ-child, and had come to the manger to worship him. Scripture says that, after seeing the babe, they went back to care for their sheep. Luther comments with a touch of humor in one of his Christmas sermons:

> This is wrong. We should correct this passage to read, "They went and shaved their heads, fasted, told their rosaries, and put on cowls." Instead we read, "The shepherds returned." Where to? To their sheep. (Roland H. Bainton, translator and arranger, *The Martin Luther Christmas Book* [Philadelphia: Muhlenberg Press, 1948], 50)

We are here today, celebrating the Reformation once again. It is not just a matter of "Here I stand!" but "Here we go!"

You now: Go back to your homes, go back to your neighbors, go back to the workplace. The sheep are waiting for you.

And if you—the church—are ready to serve a bent and broken world with the dazzling glory of an open Bible in a suffering church—then bring on the trumpets, bring on the celebrations, bring on the festivities—for by God's grace we are ready to "be witnesses unto him"—Jesus Christ, the Savior of the world!

Nothing More Beyond?
Philippians 1:23-26

[This message is adaptable also to Memorial Day weekend. It was first preached at the Minnesota South Conference, Mankato, Minnesota, on October 22, 1990.]

Centuries ago the Spanish fleet had the following inscription on their flags: *Non Plus Ultra,* "Nothing More Beyond." But then Columbus discovered America, and they had to remove the "non" from their flags. Then the flags read: *Plus Ultra,* "More Beyond." (Source unknown.)

There is "more beyond." Today we remember all the saints who have died in the Lord, and we think of the day we shall join them. There *is* more beyond. As our Lord Jesus Christ said, "I am the resurrection and the life. He who believes in Me, though he may die, he shall live. And whoever lives and believes in Me shall never die" (John 11:25-26 NKJV).

What is our stance as we still live, but knowing we will die?

In dealing with that question today, let us not only recall those who have died in the Lord, but prepare for our own death and learn to live faithfully in Christ every day.

Our text is Paul's words to the Philippians: "I am pulled in two directions. I want very much to leave this life and be with Christ, which is a far better thing; but for your sake it is much more important that I remain alive. I am sure of this, and so I know that I will stay. I will stay on with you all, to add to your progress and joy in the faith, so that when I am with you again, you will have even more reason to be proud of me in your life in union with Christ Jesus" (Phil. 1:23-26 TEV).

Those who Have Died in the Lord

On this All Saints' Day, knowing we one day will join them, we hold in blessed memory all those who have gone before us and have died in the Lord.

We recall all the saints of history: the "great cloud of witnesses" in Scripture, the Reformers, the founding fathers of our church, the greats of our own generation, and our family and friends who have died. Truly, they rest in their beds, and "their works do follow them" (Rev. 14:13 KJV). But we do not mourn, as those who have no hope. For they are in the new Jerusalem, and "He will wipe away every tear from their eyes. There will be no more death or mourning or crying or pain, for the old order of things has passed away" (Rev. 21:4)

That's why our text says, "I am pulled in two directions. I want very much to leave this life and be with Christ" and with them. Yet our separation should not obscure the fact that we are already with them—in the mystical body of Christ.

Some churches have a little semicircular communion rail around the altar. It symbolizes the great mystical union that, when we commune at that altar rail, the semicircle is completed around the throne of God in heaven. And when we chant "Hosanna, Hosanna, Hosanna," we are singing together with the whole great host around the heavenly throne. We are bound with them in one great exultant song of praise to the Lord of Life and Death. What a joy to know that circle is complete in our Eucharist together here!

Our Own Death

On this All Saints' Day, we also prepare for our own death. "I want very much to leave this life," Paul says in our text. We live eschatologically. We are ready. We prepare.

You and I are in grace. We have the sure hope of eternal life, for God has forgiven our sins through the precious, shed blood of Jesus Christ. As we say in the Gradual at the Commemoration of the Faithful Departed,

> I love the Lord, for he heard my voice; he heard my cry for mercy. Because he turned his ear to me, I will call on him as long as I live. He has caused his wonders to be remembered; the Lord is gracious and compassionate. Show me, O Lord, my life's end and the number of my days. (*Lutheran Worship*, 105)

That was the Apostle Paul's point in our text. He knew his days were numbered, but he was prepared. So are we to be ready, to prepare. As one pastor announced after a prayer for a recently deceased fellow pastor, "And now let us pray for the next one among us who will die."

On another occasion, an old-time prairie preacher in his 80s was in the hospital preparing to die. He sent his son to his study at home and had him bring the file on his own funeral. His son by his bed, the old pastor asked, "Do you have a pen and paper?" "Yes," said the son as he waited for his father's last words. It was a sacred moment.

"Go out to the garage," he said huskily, "and take all the cans and bottles down to the garbage dump. Go south on Hydraulic, turn left just after you cross the bridge ..." In his last hours he still was concerned about putting his house in order. After that, though, the veteran pastor went on to give his son the text for his funeral service, the hymns ("I Know that My Redeemer Liveth" and "Lamb of God, We Bow before Thee"), and the officiants. Having made a strong declaration of his faith in our Lord Jesus Christ, who died for us and rose again, he directed his tombstone to read, "I know whom I have believed." (*Bound to Be Free*, 53–54)

In like manner, you and I are to watch and pray, to be ready at all times. The early Christians always lived in imminent expectation of our Lord's return—and so should we, as the Book of Revelation ends, "He who testifies to these things says, 'Yes, I am coming soon.' Amen. Come, Lord Jesus" (Rev. 22:20).

Living Faithfully

On this All Saints' Day as we look at the death of others and of ourselves, we also look at our *lives,* for we live day by day with Jesus. Paul says, "I am pulled in two directions ... but I will stay on with you all." So we live daily in expectation of our death, yet live each day knowing it will never come again.

A young pastor once interviewed an elderly pastor about his life. After an hour of listening, the interviewer finally asked quietly, "What do you think about your death?" The veteran of the cross paused for a moment and then said slowly, "Well, I do not fear it; I trust in the Lord." Then he added with a twinkle in his eye, "But I am not courting death, either!" (Personal comment to the author.)

A real estate salesman who had open heart surgery says he now begins every day with the exultation, "Thank you, Lord, for another day!" (Personal comment to the author.)

And there was a college student who each evening would pull the curtain and say, "Perhaps tonight, Lord?" And in the morning he would pull back the curtain and say, "Perhaps today, Lord?" (Source unknown.)

We live as those who know they will die, but we live with a zest and vividness and detachment, for we know we will not pass this way again. We face our end with conviction knowing whom we believe, and we are persuaded with "he is able to guard what I have entrusted to him for that day" (2 Tim. 1:12).

So that is our task on this All Saints' Day: 1) We recall those who have died in the Lord; 2) We prepare for our own death; and 3) We live faithfully in the Lord—in Christ—each and every day.

How do we continue to do that in the face of often over-whelming odds in our lives?

No doubt you've read of the 500-mile dogsled race over a part of Minnesota. The same lady who won in 1987 also won in 1988. We're talking about a pioneer woman! She pressed on through bitter cold, the howling winds of a blizzard, dark nights, and exhausting days, as her well-trained huskies pulled her sled over those hundreds of miles from the start to the finish of the race. The dogs were fitted with little socks over their paws since the ice resembles sandpaper after so many miles. It can literally rip the pads off their feet. Though strong and in great condition, the struggling animals with those little socks on their feet barked, pulled, and pressed on despite the odds.

Another woman, Susan Butcher, three times in a row won the 1,100-mile Iditarod race from Anchorage to Nome. Ten to twelve days in the middle of nowhere. Maddening monotony. Strain beyond belief.

How do they do it? I can tell you part of the answer. One of the women said, "I just remembered that others have done it before me, so I can do it, too." (Adapted from Charles Swindoll, *The Quest for Character* [Portland: Multnomah, 1987], 175)

This is not to give you a moralistic injunction for your Christian life which merely says "You can do it, so try harder."

Rather, I say, those faithful Christians who have gone before you relied not on their own strength while they lived, but as Paul said of his own life, "Our competence comes from God" (2 Cor. 3:5).

We are tempted at times to think that God doesn't care or doesn't know what's going on in our lives. It's like some of those "informatory" prayers we hear at times, "O Lord, you know we've got problems in our congregation, you know we've got problems in our city, in our state." To which a friend responded, "What's the matter, don't you think the Lord reads the newspaper?"

That's often our problem: We are not sure about God's interest in us. But the fact that God is silent does not mean there is no God. "The absence of evidence is not evidence of absence" for the Christian. Our "hidden" God is also our God revealed in Scripture and in the person of Jesus Christ.

Rev. John Soundajarian, originally from India, tells this story.

An old Christian lady had a dream like this. In her dream she saw three others at prayer, praying to God to deliver them out of their troubles and sufferings. As they were praying, the Master drew near to them. As he approached the first of the three, he bent over her in tenderness and grace, with smiles full of radiant love and spoke to her in accents of purest, sweetest music. Leaving her, he came to the next, but only placed his hand upon her bowed head, and gave her one look of loving approval. The third woman he passed almost abruptly without stopping for a word or glance.

The woman in her dream said to herself, "How greatly he must love the first one! To the second he gave his approval, but none of the special demonstrations of love he gave the first. And the third must have grieved him deeply, for he gave her no word at all and not even a passing look. I wonder at what she has done, and why he made so much difference between them."

As she tried to account for the action of her Lord, he himself stood by her and said, "O woman! How wrongly you have interpreted me. The first kneeling woman needs all the weight of my tenderness and care to keep her feet in my narrow way. She needs my love, thought, and help every moment of the day. Without it she would fail and fall. The second has stronger faith and deeper love, and I can trust her to trust me however things may go and whatever people do.

"The third, whom I seemed not to notice and even to neglect, has faith and love of the finest quality, and I am training her by quick and drastic processes for the highest and holiest service. She knows me so intimately and trusts me so utterly that she is independent of words or looks or any outward intimation of my approval. She is not dismayed nor discouraged by any circumstances through which I arrange that she shall pass; she trusts me when sense and reason and every finer instinct of the natural heart would rebel; because she knows that I am working in her for eternity, and that what I do, though she knows not the explanation now, she will understand hereafter. I am silent in my love beyond the power of words to express. Also I am silent in my love for your sakes that you may learn to love and trust." (Adapted from Charles E. Cowman, *Streams in the Desert* [Vepery, Madras, India: Evangelistic Literature Service, 1982], 44-45)

What a great God you and I have—who is always there for you, even when he is seemingly silent!

"I will never leave you nor forsake you," he says.

On this All Saints' Day, you have not yet joined the blessed dead whom you remember this day. But your own death can come at any time.

Oh, may you, like them, be always faithful, knowing the Lord is at your side. And may you, as you live, and when you die, exult in the blessed certainty that there is more beyond.